YOUR HALF OF THE APPLE

God &
The Single Girl

gini andrews

foreword
by
Francis Schaeffer

ZONDERVAN
PUBLISHING HOUSE

OF THE ZONDERVAN CORPORATION
GRAND RAPIDS, MICHIGAN 49506

To
NANCY

YOUR HALF OF THE APPLE
© 1972 by The Zondervan Corporation
Grand Rapids, Michigan

ISBN 0-310-20171-3

Library of Congress Catalog Card Number 72-189574

Printed in the United States of America

83 84 85 86 87 88 — 20 19

Contents

Foreword

With the collapse of the Northern European culture which rested upon the Reformation, men and women at the end of the twentieth century are faced with many practical results in every field, but nowhere more than in the field of morals, and certainly in sexual morals and attitudes.

It is easy to be infiltrated (unwittingly) by these new attitudes simply because we are surrounded by such a united voice concerning them. When Kinsey wrote, he seemed very far out, and most people really did not understand the central thing of importance concerning him. The central thing was not that he reported statistics in the sexual practices of a certain number of men and women, but that he was a prominent voice presenting a relativistic concept concerning sex. That is, that what is right is what the average of a certain society is doing in sexual things at that given moment. A country like Sweden now operates in sexual things upon this base. And in practice it is exactly what has happened in the United States and Britain as well.

When men turn away from the infinite-personal God and what He teaches in the Bible of that which conforms to His character, one of the first outward places where it shows is in the area of sexual things. And I think it is because the man-woman relationship as God made it is the second strongest drive man has. The first is the need of the finite creature, man, to be in relationship with the infinite-personal God who is there, who exists—not only for theoretical answers, but for the fulfillment of man as God made him uniquely in contrast to non-man. It is certainly evident that the revolt of man against God quickly shows up in sexual abnormalities and sexual sorrows. It was true in the Old Testament times, it was true in the

Greek-Roman culture, and it is true today. The double tragedy is that when man does this, he is not only doing what is wrong, but he also is injured because God made him to be fulfilled in a certain way, and when man tries to find his sexual fulfillment in other ways, he is not fulfilled. He is functioning on a lower level than God meant for him both in fulfillment and in joy.

On the other hand, we must realize that a platonic element has tended to creep into Evangelical Christianity which has nothing to do with the teaching of the Bible. This shows itself in the suspicion that if a person is interested in intellectual or cultural problems, this must indicate that he is not really interested in spiritual ones. This, of course, is wrong, for God made the whole man and true spirituality involves the whole man, including the reason and the creative desires God has put within man as made in God's image. Nowhere, however, do platonic elements show themselves more clearly than in sexual things. Christianity is constantly between two non-biblical concepts. First, asceticism, and secondly, antinomianism. Asceticism is really platonic and not biblical. It means a feeling and teaching that it is intrinsically good not to be fulfilled in the bodily, intellectual, and cultural pleasures for which God made man before the Fall. Antinomianism is the opposite teaching—that after a man is a Christian, he can live without being bound by the propositional commands of Scripture. Both are equally pernicious and unbiblical.

Today, as our culture is disintegrating, there really is "death in the city" in the total society. In the sexual areas only relativism is left, and the whole concept, as in the area of technology, is that there is only one boundary condition—namely, that we should do everything we can do. In both technology and sexual things modern man has no base for a second boundary condition of what he *should* do in the light of all the things that he can do. In sexual things, as in technological, we constantly see young people who began on this road when they were eight, nine, or ten years of age and who now are destroyed sexually because they have done everything. They have functioned on a purely animal level, rather than in the area where love is different from sex and where the sex relationship is a vehicle for that unique love and communication which is possible in the man-woman relationship. Not only are they destroyed morally, but they also are destroyed as human beings, and they are destroyed in the unique wonder and pleasure of human sex.

We must have courage to accept the fact that our culture has become Sodom and Gomorrah, and we cannot blame it only on the young. The young people have taken the drug culture and open promiscuous sex to a new intensity, but as John Updike rightly points out in his book *Couples*, the previous generation who hid these things from public view were really hung up on alcoholism and adultery. Thus it is not merely the younger generation that must think through these things, but the older, middle-class generation with its memory of a Christian past and yet inward and practicing hypocrisy.

It will take more than some romantic, half-hidden presentation to meet this infiltration. In order to confront it, we must be as tough fibered as were the prophets, who under the inspiration of the Holy Spirit spoke with frankness and firmness of these things amidst the moral breakdown of their day. Our speaking must be with equal frankness or it will be useless before the world of our day and before the needs of our own children. If there is to be an answer to *The Sensuous Woman* and other books like it, we must have the courage to speak as the prophets spoke. And speak we must, or we are unfaithful to the Scripture, unfaithful to the wounded world which surrounds us, and unfaithful to our own children as they are faced with titanic pressures. — *Francis A. Schaeffer*

I

It Started With Eve

So you want to get married?

What a question! Who doesn't?

But here you are: 23, 28, 35, even 40 or 45, and you're not. And you resent it.

O.K. To begin with, let's admit one thing: most women want marriage, but some won't make it. There are a variety of reasons, one of the more depressing being statistics: 109 women to every 100 men, is it? Facing these grim realities, what's a Christian girl going to do? How is she going to act — and react?

Marriage is good; it's great. Woman was created by God to be man's helper and complement, to be his fulfillment and he to be hers. God's original plan was to have the personalities complement each other on the human stratum; marriage, as

He intended it, is ideal.

Hooray! I like this!

But came the Fall and many things went wrong. Men and women wrenched the reins of their individual lives out of God's hands; sin and disease and twisted personalities were the result. Now you of the twentieth century are faced with a multitude of problems in this area that were never in the original plan. You face these questions:

Is marriage the *only* answer?

Is it the *best* answer?

Is it the best answer for *you*?

If for some reason it's not, how are you to handle this and live with real fulfillment, verve, and excitement? Or is this asking too much? Can God give you a full, rich life without marriage?

Let's turn that sentence around and say (read it aloud, why don't you?):

God cannot give me a full, rich life without marriage.

He can't?

What kind of God have we? What about the thousands of women today who know this is not true? Are you sure you've made a clear distinction between your own desire for yourself, social pressure as to what life should be, and God's plan for your life?

Oh no! Not another dreary book about being God's little sunbeam and spreading sweetness and light. I can't stand it!

Hold it! Unhand that wastebasket for a few minutes, please.

If the phrase, "God's plan for your life," conjures up a picture of a dumpy dame with bad skin and a wardrobe straight out of the missionary barrel, you and I aren't talking about the same God. So hang on, won't you?

Maybe we'd better begin all this at the real beginning: With God.

You can, of course, skip over to the chapters on things that may seem more vital and interesting: clothes, dating, and that never-exhausted subject — sex. Be my guest. But a lot of that won't make much sense if you don't understand the framework in which it is said.

If you're still thinking of God as an outdated, rather fuddy-duddy Authority Figure who's fine for such things as salvation and help in great trials, but really quite inexperienced when it comes to the Big Things that have to do with being young and LIVING LIFE, then we're really *not* talking about the same God. It's only as, and if, you see God as completely contemporary, completely understanding of You as a whole being, as a Person who cares about You: your loneliness, your fears of old-maid-ness, your insecurities with men, with life, your dateless Saturday nights, your looks and what you can do about them — only if He is that real and that concerned will you be able to relate this vital problem of unwilling singleness to Christian life. Without a God who is involved, we have no mooring, to say nothing of no heart-response.

It was all His plan from the first, you know. Sometimes I think we get the idea that we have to struggle in this area on our own; that if we dare invite God in on the control of this phase of our lives, He'll accept our great sacrifice (accept? demand!), and off we'll go in flat brogans and a sacky suit, in the most unbecoming hair-do imaginable to the most unattractive part of the world we can think of: Eskimo-land, or, if you hate heat, it's bound to be India.

Why not look at some instances in the Bible where God had a definite hand in the romance?

Ever stop to think how gorgeous Eve must have been? Remember, that was before sin and aging and deformities, before the need for diets, glasses, and girdles. She was God's perfect design, and she was stunning. The love and companionship Adam and she shared must have been the greatest romance the world has ever known. Why? It was God-planned.

Does God understand the closeness of the relationship we feel for the man we love or would like to love? He took Eve out of Adam's body; *He* did it. He made her for man, and that day as they faced each other there was a unique complementing of two beings: physically, emotionally, spiritually. This was God's design.

And perhaps right here is the place to say that *I do* accept the Genesis story, along with the rest of the Bible, as God's revelation. I do believe God has spoken to mankind: "He declares unto man His thought." Our Christian faith stands or falls with the inspiration of Scripture. I'm writing to you as Christian girls and women with the assumption that you need no convincing that God exists, that He is both infinite and personal, and that Jesus Christ is the Eternal Son of God who came to give His life for your redemption. However, some of you, perhaps many of you, have been battered by modern philosophy or non-philosophy, confused by skim-milk theology, brainwashed at universities, or simply have never had a *foundation* for what you've been taught about the Bible at home and in church. I would urge you to re-examine this exciting book. *Is* it God's revelation? *Does* it speak to you twentieth-century girls? Is it speaking truth about history where it touches history, about men in general and you in particular, about the universe that you see all around you and about which science has been making such titanic discoveries? Have you really challenged this book on your own, or have you ditched part of it on someone else's say-so? If it's what Christianity has always claimed for it: the revelation of God's thoughts and *words* to mankind, it's both worthy of investigation and it can afford to be investigated. It can stand any question your bright, modern mind can put to it!

Back to the First Lady:

We know what happened next in the story, but keep in mind that the suffering (and the arguments and misunderstandings that undoubtedly came up between Mr. and Mrs. Adam) was definitely not God's idea.

What about subsequent romances in Biblical history?

There was Rebecca. Abraham's servant prayed, and Isaac seems to have married an outstanding girl. She was "very fair," she was courteous and thoughtful, and she had a deep-rooted personal faith in God which must have been developed well before Abraham's servant came along.

Jacob slaved seven years for one woman, had another palmed off on him by a matchmaking father, and then worked another seven years for the girl of his choice! How's that for devotion?

David's life story certainly contrasts the good and the bad in his relationships with women, doesn't it? When he waited for God's timing, he did all right (Abigail being a case in point), but when he took matters into his own hands, he really got into trouble.

God took Moses' part in his interracial marriage with the Ethiopian lady; and Joseph's wife must have been quite a woman because Joseph was in a scene where he could have had his pick and polygamy was rife, yet as far as we're told he had only this one partner.

I love Esther's story: There she goes, Miss Persia, number-one girl to an all-powerful Oriental potentate who loved her very much. (It's not mentioned whether or not she loved him, but she certainly had her priorities straight when she risked her lovely neck going unsummoned to this unpredictable man who had jettisoned the first queen because of her disobedience.) Notice how he promised Esther whatever she asked for: "unto the half of my kingdom" (and that was a lot of real estate), before he even found out what this girl-queen of his wanted.

The whole Song of Solomon is a paean of praise to human romantic love, and surely, if God didn't approve the *whole* of man's love for woman, He would hardly have included that in the Bible?

What about Ruth? After some lonely and bitter struggles with her singleness, this lady learned how to put first things first, and as a result became part of the direct line which brought forth the Messiah.

Of course, the most compelling argument for God's approval of the marriage relationship is in His definite New Testament instructions about it, emphasizing love, tenderness, and consideration, but even more: equating this relationship with Christ and the believer. It's exciting to think that God isn't saying, "Oh, yes, you may use this human experience as an illustration of the Christ-believer relationship," but that He *designed* marriage to express the inexpressible closeness into which He would bring you and me with our living Lord.

Fine. Great. God approves of marriage and romance — so do I! But I'M single: What's wrong with me? I'm the stigmatized swan, the hollyhock at the dance. I'm living in Vancouver, Colorado Springs, London, San Francisco. No rich fathers I know are sending out servants to select wives for young heirs. I'm not a winner in an oriental beauty contest. I'm not even Miss Sunflower Junction, and I dare you to show me one man who'd work seven years at anything for any girl, let alone me. What's God going to do about ME?

Right.

Human beings having been human beings since history started, I don't suppose Rebecca was very different from most of you. She probably put her hair up every night and felt that living on Daddy Bethuel's farm didn't give her much chance to find a man — and who wants to be watering sheep forever? But she also seems to have been learning to know

16

God: notice how complete and unquestioning her trust was when the crunch came.

How exciting is your relationship with the Lord? Maybe you don't think excitement either possible or practical. Think of the traits you love in people: gentleness, imagination, tenderness, warmth, understanding — to name only a few. Now realize that God is *infinite* in each of these areas. The Bible is bursting with references to support this.

Or take humor. Surely you don't visualize God without a sense of humor? What about some of the delightful animals there are: a pair of electronic kittens, a bumbling puppy, or just the size and shape of some monkeys? Do you really think a humorless God could create the marvelously comic imaginations that have sparkled through the centuries?

The best of the lovable and heartwarming qualities you see in people you love are sparks struck from the great conflagration of His beauty. Is He more wonderful, more exciting, more real than anyone you know in your everyday life? If He is not, then, lady, you're missing out; you really are.

Whatever other solutions there may be to bring you a more joyous life of fulfillment and alleviate your loneliness, whether you remain single or get married, this is the real heart of the matter. *In no way* am I suggesting to you that a deep relationship with the Lord is something that will tide you over till The Man comes into your life. It's not a protem thing at all. It's not a question of: "Dear Lord, hold my hand; take me through this experience of singleness somehow," and then, if romance arrives, dropping that hand and rushing gaily to the altar shouting, "Thanks, Lord; now I can start LIVING!" Not at all. Before any other purpose, you were made for God; ". . . in the image of God created He *them.*"

We will never know all that God intended us to know of real challenge in life, the *joie de vivre* which is part, not all, of the Christian experience, if we don't reach a point where we experience God's reality in a deeply warm and personal way. Surely this is part of what Paul was trying to say in the much-quoted thirteenth chapter of First Corinthians? You can have zeal burning you up and a Phi Beta Kappa key to boot, but without love it's ashes.

Love! Yeh!! Lead me to it! That's just what I want. She doesn't need to sell me on that!

Do you love God? Warmly? Real heart response?

W...e...l...l....

And remember, this love can no more be whipped up, turned-on, manufactured than the falling-in-love kind can.

Then what...?

You *learn* to love a human being by being with him, spending time getting to know what he's like. It's a living, growing thing even in marriage. You talk and you listen; you think about one another a lot.

God thinking about me? The world, sure; mankind, yes, but... me?

David said, "How precious also are thy thoughts unto me, O God .... If I should count them, they are more in number than the sand"; and in another place: "we are ever in Your thoughts." Do you think David was more precious to God than you are? Our God doesn't go by protocol; He doesn't have favorites; He loves *each* of His children. The importance of the individual runs like a leitmotif throughout the whole Bible; the titanic implications of the choices of one man have come crashing down through history since Adam set his will against his Creator. Ever since that time God has been lovingly pointing out the value of one person to Him: "I have called thee by *thy name*." "Ruth, Nancy, Jeanie,

18

Elaine, Susie, Bonnie, Karen . . ." — not a long serial number in the heavenly census. "*You* are Mine." *One* sheep, *one* sinner that repents. "I call my own sheep *by name*." (And don't you love that intimate verse in Revelation 2:17: the white stone given with the new name which no one knows but him to whom it is given — just you and God — some special secret between you and your Lord, perhaps a souvenir of some struggle, some triumph in your life, and His forgiveness for your failure!)

What does He think of you? This is what He thinks of you — you in your office in midtown Manhattan, your schoolroom in Butte, Montana, your hospital in Montreal — whoever you are or wherever, He says to you:

So precious are you to Me — *So* honored — *So* beloved.
I have graven *you* on the palms of My hands.
He that touches *you* touches the apple of My eye.
As the Father has loved Me, *so* have I loved *you*.

These for a start; there are hundreds more.

Is this woman trying to sell me some kind of Pollyanna malarky to take my mind off the big hunger for human love and a home?

No, lady, she's not. The need in all of us for human love is monumental. I spent many years as a single girl, and am now single again, and I know something about loneliness, about frustration, and, yes, about the anger against God who, it seemed, would not do for me what I kept asking Him to do. If in the past I'd known more of His deeply personal caring for me, if I had understood Him better, known more what He is really like, I'd have avoided a lot of pain and a lot of the plain and fancy mistakes I managed over the years. I would have saved a lot of time and would have had a far finer life to look back on than I now have.

The real core of the matter is our relationship with the infinite Almighty God. If this brings no sense of excitement, we're not plugged in somewhere.

Now wait a minute! I know God. I've been a Christian for years! I've accepted Christ as my Savior; I teach Sunday school classes; I belong to all the youth groups. Why I'm a leader of the . . . .

Good. But are you excited about God? Do you find His love *real?*

It's my enviable privilege to talk with many girls, mainly in the 18-25 age group, and I've seen any number of these sharp kids — good-looking, lively — really brimming over about God. If someone talks to you about God as an infinitely wonderful Person, about the beauty of the Lord, does this ring any bells at all or does it sound awfully romantic and far-out?

What about *your* response to God's love? Of course, if you don't understand how much He loves you, that's not apt to be very positive, is it? I know you girls: you're warm and vital and outgoing to human love. I see you coming into my room with the most beautiful gestures of caring: a cup of coffee, flowers, or just with shining eyes to say hello. I see you with each other, with some deeply confused contemporary, with someone who's obnoxious because he's hurting inside and you see this and treat him with the most exquisite gentleness. But if you have no real heart response to this God we're talking about, no wonder you find it difficult, even impossible, to trust Him with this deeply personal area of your life as a woman: finding a mate or going without one. Why *should* you let a stranger run your life? You cannot admit someone you hardly know into the sanctum sanctorum of your inner self, especially if you're not sure He understands that self at all. If you've never proved Him in lesser areas: choice of schools, vacations, dates, lost articles, stuck zippers, how can you give Him your *heart?* He wants to be proved, you know: "Prove me now . . . if I will not . . . pour you out a blessing." A little blessing? Something to tide you over a bit? "That there shall not be room enough to receive it!" He is the giving God. He allowed Gideon to prove Him with that really outrageous request about the fleece, not once, but twice.

O.K. Maybe I don't know Him so well. How do I go about this?

How do you get to know anyone? Try listing the ways. As a start: you meet him; then you have to spend time with him, talking (but also listening); you find out what he likes, what he's been through. If it's an attractive man you're talking with, you can't (if you're smart) get enough of his telling you about *his* interests, *his* exploits, *his* hopes, and *his* dreams. If he's one of those rare males who writes, you devour his letters. If you meet a famous painter or composer, you learn much from just examining his work. Watch that new boyfriend with other people; watch him with children or old people; you'll see a side that's different from the one he shows you. Of course, it takes *time* to know someone well — time and — wanting to. Translate some of these ideas into the area of getting to know your Heavenly Father; I think you'll find it opens up some exciting doors.

Yours is a God who cares for you in detail, who wants to be *involved* in all you do. He is truly interested in whether or not you pass that exam, find the great new outfit for that date, or — well, there's just nothing about you He *doesn't* care about. How many hairs in that nice head of hair on which you spend so much time? You don't know, do you? He does. If God notices a sparrow fall, do you think He doesn't care when you burn a cake, wreck the new nylons, or lose a boyfriend? He cares so much that you can hurt His feelings. "Grieve not the holy Spirit of God." Grieve is a love word: you can anger someone who doesn't love you; you can grieve only someone who cares. He says: "I drench you with My tears." Have you thought about the Almighty shedding tears over *you*? What are you doing about loving Him back?

21

The love relationship between you and your God is *forever*. It's not just till marriage and not just till death either. The intimacy and comradeship begun here is being forged every day as a link in the chain of a *permanent* relationship, so permanent that it's eternal. This warm marvelous tie has in it no good-bys, no separations, no vacations, no times of alienation unless we choose to become alienated. Even so, *He's* always the same and runs to meet us as we fumble our way back to Him.

Loving and radiant, He goes with you on the subway to work, into the kitchen when you're tired, with you as you open the door of your lonely room at night; He can surround you like a warm, white light at the end of the day.

The struggle to find balance between God's utter sufficiency in our lives and the need He has created in us for our own kind is not easy. We scream inside for understanding, the perfect complement, for one in whom we will feel totally fulfilled and at rest; yet we *must* face the hard fact that *never* will we find this total completeness in a merely human relationship. As Christians we know this in our heads, but all too often down on "gut level" we don't accept it; so we go deeper and deeper in our despondency as we seek it and fail to find it. Then we start feeling mad at God for not understanding our needs and *doing* something about them; and all the time He stands there, knowing that only He can satisfy the bottomless cravings of our hearts, longing to do just that.

Marilyn Monroe has been quoted as saying that all her life had been a search for limitless love. Now, according to the standards of many, she had everything it takes to get just that: looks, sex-appeal that wouldn't quit, money, fame, opportunity unlimited; yet her end was a tragic negation of this.

The romantic ladies of history all sought it, didn't they? Cleopatra, Mary Queen of Scots, Eleanor of Aquitaine. And there would be no opera without Tosca, Mimi, Carmen,

Manon — these searchers-after-limitless-love. But think about the end in *all* these stories: did they find it? *Is* there limitless love anywhere?

Isn't this what you are searching for: unlimited love, understanding, and approval? Oh, you're a realist; you know there's nothing perfect, but deep inside you there's the hope that someday you'll find one person, just one, who will give you the love and understanding for which your heart hungers.

Well, can't a good marriage, a good Christian marriage bring limitless love? Shouldn't it?

How much weight can a human relationship bear? There is the danger of our destroying the whole structure, of making a man feel trapped, futile, a failure because we want him to fill *all* the longings of our heart.

Then do we just go on with these empty places in us, the secret lonelinesses, the lacks that wake us up in the night or make us cringe inside when we see someone who has what we want?

There *is* limitless love — a love that's *always* there, always yours, always completely understanding and accepting, but it's only on the divine level, never on the human. God wants to give it to you, but He will never force it on you; like His creatures, He waits to be wanted.

Does this mean we have no need for human companionship, human love, for marriage? Of course not. But I wonder if He sometimes waits till we experience the cavernous size of the emptiness in us (far too big for any mere human being to fill) before He allows us to be distracted from the main issue by satisfying our lesser needs.

This is the Biggest Thing life has to offer: a deeply personal, day-by-day, hour-to-hour love relationship with the living God, and it's as freely available to you as to your married sisters. Everything beautiful in life enhances this, but *nothing* replaces it.

2

Going WHOSE Way ?

Maybe you're mad at God because you're single? I used to be.

Have you thought about His conditions for a fulfilled life?

Conditions? What's she nattering about now? There are conditions?

Christ said: "Seek ye *first* the kingdom of God, and his righteousness; and all these things shall be added unto you." Now if this God cares so much about you, where will He fit in your priorities? Do you feel, guiltily, that — well, He *should* be at the top, knowing full well He is not? If this is so, isn't it again because you don't really understand what He's like?

This is the God who became a Man, sunburned and strong, who struggled with weariness and hunger, thirst and heat, with the stinking, disease-ridden mob around Him all the time, and who finally died in agony because you were — and are — important to Him. If you're beginning to see Him, maybe you're ready to think about your life, goals, and ambitions in relation to this wonderful Person.

You with your tender responses underneath the flip exterior: can you refuse to love Him? Does He have the right-of-way in your choices? Coming down to the nitty-gritty: are you your own girl?

This is beginning to read like a sermon. When is she going to get to the meat in the coconut? What about me as a solo act when I want to be part of a duet?

You may see yourself as a single girl struggling to find her identity and achingly wanting that identity to be *Mrs.* Somebody. God is interested in you as a person, a *whole* person, an individual of unique design. No one else in all the world is just like you; no one else in all of history has ever been just like you, and your response to God is precious to Him. It is a one-of-a-kind relationship. Your identity is, first of all, as a marvelous being God Himself has made for fellowship with Himself forever. Your future is wonderful, and He wants you to live in day-by-day consciousness of this and enjoy your heritage as a daughter of the great King.

Not fantasy. Fact.

Are you more concerned about finding a man than you are about finding God's plan for you? Isn't that putting the well-known cart before the timeworn horse?

But I'm hoping God's plan includes the right man and . . . .

How can you ever recognize the right man if you haven't asked the All-Knowing who designed you what *He* plans to make of your life? How can you go about finding the man He has picked out for you if you don't ask Him what you should become and where you should go? Suppose God plans for you to be at Rosewood College and, without asking, you chug off to Updown University. Meanwhile, Your Hero has showed up at Rosewood (as God knew he would), while at dear old Updown you're screaming, "Why doesn't God *do* something?"

If God really is your Lord, your Sovereign, it's imperative for you to discover *His* goal for you. You're His very own; far from being uninterested, He's passionately interested in whatever you do, where you go, what becomes of you. He has *chosen* you, picked you out for a whole exciting life on this planet — a life of companionship and joy with Himself. Marriage can be a part, but the goal, God's goal for you, is that you "bear the family likeness of His Son." He has chosen *you* to the "splendor of life as His own" daughter, and this is a *guarantee* that His choices for you will be for your fulfillment, happiness, and wholeness. Do you know anywhere else you can get a lifetime guarantee like that? (Let's interject here that I'm not being unrealistic and saying that the Christian life — married or single — is one long, posy-strewn pathway; it most definitely is *not*. But come on, do you know of any route through life that is? Look around.)

When all is said and done, isn't the crux of the whole matter one of our main goal, our key purpose in life? As Christian women, we are like our non-Christian sisters in so many respects: emotionally, physically, with the same basic needs, drives, and problems.

But — and here is where the Christian girl or woman adds an enormous plus on her half of the ledger.

But: We have a different life. Not a different life-style (though we should have that, too), but we have the life of Christ Himself. What we are becoming is just a foretaste of the extension of the life we are now living. You will still be you in the New Life; you're not going to become someone totally other than you are now. Perfected, certainly, but the life of Christ that is in you today is the same as that which you will experience (sans hindrances, sin, and limitations) when you continue on into His Presence. Because of this, we have different goals than our non-Christian sisters. Our ambition is to please Him, to express a little of the gratitude we feel for having been brought into right relationship with the God of all the earth, for having been given total forgiveness through the death of Christ, total acceptance in the Beloved. Our ambition should be to demonstrate in our life-style that there is more to life than the acquisition of things, than getting our place in the sun, even than just "living the good life," whatever that may mean specifically to each of us. Our aim is to exhibit so much of the love of Christ that people will be drawn, not to us, but to Him and find in Him the answers to their own deepest longings.

Our priorities are different: while social life, friends, dates, husband-to-be, careers all have a valued place in our lives, what God wants for us and of us is of prime importance to us. For Him, the glorious, eternal God, there rightfully can be only one place in our hearts and in our lives: First. It's a question of "seeing Him who is invisible," isn't it?

What have we lined up in the way of priorities?

1. Discovering what God is really like.
2. Discovering what God thinks about you.
3. Discovering God's goal for your individual life.

We need to keep in mind that God made Himself vulnerable the day He gave man the power to choose. He is still vulnerable; you are still free to choose not to choose His way. Isn't this a tremendous statement on the significance of the individual?

Well, yes, but does God's goal include marriage for me — and when, when, when?

Does God know as much as you do? Are you willing to trust Him enough to put yourself, your whole self, into His charge and go forward with real excitement into the future He has for you, telling Him as often as you like that you *want* love, you *want* a home and husband and kids, but you're on your way on the route He wants you to go, that you understand that He really *does* know how to make you happy?

What about this two-plane living into which we fall? You know: the spiritual life, the devotional life, our Christianity is up on this plane, and then below — there's *life!* And seldom the twain shall meet. This is part of our trouble in allowing God to invade *all* the areas of our lives. Does this dichotomy actually exist for the Christian?

Isn't it true for many of us that we compartmentalize our lives? There's the Sunday Life: Sunday school (with the lesson worked on in the car en route to the church), then church, *maybe* a youth group on Sunday evening or the Sunday evening service. By Sunday night we are just about ready to sprout wings.

Comes Monday A.M.: The alarm goes off with a sleep-splintering shock; we stagger, muttering, out of bed; we groan, *"Monday!"*; and suddenly *we* are in the driver's seat of our lives, and off we go through a week of frantic activity which includes our job, errands, meetings, and social engagements. That God might be interested or would care to have some say in our decisions does not enter our minds; this is *our* department. Oh, in a crisis we'll pray madly, but —. Is it possible that had we asked our Father's advice, the crisis might never have occurred?

Is there really a "secular" side to the Christian life? Brother Lawrence, working day after day in a medieval kitchen, didn't think so, and whatever his mundane tasks, he did them as a sacrament for his God. We can take this attitude; we can also realize that routine things have real potential for learning about God. At the Laundromat, the grocery store, or in a neighborhood kaffee klatsch we may find someone hungry to hear whether there are any answers to life's problems. (Let me quickly say, I am *not* advocating button-holing every person you meet, or for that matter *any* person you meet, with: "Are you a Christian? If not, why not?") What I do mean is that we can go on our day's appointments asking God to lead us to some seeking mind, and we can have some exciting times even in a railway station or at a lunch counter. Be wide-open; life gets exciting this way, and the ordinary lanes down which we go can lead to adventure. I'm not being romantic; I've seen it happen.

Ever include God in your shopping?

Now wait a minute! Let's not get ridiculous! That's really far out.

Not really. Next time you go shopping, ask Him to help you find the right dress, or the new car, or even the gloves you had in mind. You may be surprised at what good taste He has and find you've spent far less money than you'd feared.

I suppose He knows, but how can I bother Almighty God with my silly little affairs? Isn't this what He's given me a mind for? Besides, He has bigger things on His mind.

He has indeed, but you are dealing with the God who is infinite. It's no problem for Him to deal with the stars and the seasons and angels and nations and at the same time give you His loving attention every day, twenty-four hours, three-hundred-and-sixty-five days of every year. It's no strain on His resources to keep up with everything that concerns any of His children everywhere at once, and He cares about *you*.

As Christian girls and women, what should our goal be? In the words of the old Westminster Confession, man is created to:

1. glorify God
2. enjoy Him forever.

Sound dreary? I have a young friend whose hackles rise at the mere idea that she is here to glorify God. Maybe yours do too?

What kind of goal is that for this day and age?

When anything is created for a specific purpose, it's not really complete unless it's being used *for* that purpose. Take a diamond necklace: gleaming on the black velvet in a jeweler's window it's beautiful, desirable, but cooly impersonal. Now put it on the neck of a lovely woman; place her, dressed in a Paris original, at a candlelit dinner table, and the picture becomes complete; the jewels are as they are supposed to be: ornamenting and enhancing a person who is warm, vibrant, living. Last year I had my first look at the crown jewels of England. I had seen detailed pictures in color, but I was not prepared for the flaming radiance I saw in the Tower of London, the stabbing spears of colored fire. Yet only on the head of the living sovereign do they fulfill what they were made for and become part of a whole great tradition, symbolic of many things. In a sense these gems glorify the individual wearing them, and yet in no sense do they forfeit one iota of their individuality. Many times in the Bible God uses jewels to express both our value and our relationship to Himself. You are a jewel of infinite value to be set as a blazing ornament for the King of Kings. Single or married, this is your highest purpose.

Then that second phrase: to enjoy Him forever. If you're not *enjoying* Him, if there's not a vital communication going on between you and the King, if you're outside in the waiting room somewhere and not in the audience chamber, you're being cheated — and *God* never does the cheating; He's the Giving God.

How about it? *Have* you a goal? Does your life have any overall pattern, any direction? What are you living for day after day? On what are you expending your energy, time, and money? Are you just getting, by, struggling through somehow, frustrated and brain-weary, hoping tomorrow will be better, the weekend will bring some new kick, the summer a break in the routine? Is *this* the abundant life Christ talked about?

But I have very definite goals.

Good. Now, next question: Are they *His* goals for you? Had you thought of God having a particular goal for your life, a niche for your particular talents? It's a big thought when we first realize that He has created us with something particular in mind and that He has the right to choose for us, whether it be a mate, a career, or even the better of two appointments. ("Little" decisions often lead to mammoth changes in our lives.) He does not force His claim; we are always free to choose our own route or His. He wants to go over plans with you, to be "in" on your thinking. Are you sure you're going His way, or have you been heading down a path of your own choosing, asking Him to bless it before finding out if it is *His* path? Perhaps if you will stop now and listen, He is waiting to show you a far better plan.

To give Him some time in "Christian service," to be busy at church, Sunday school, or committee meetings, to tell others about Him — are these your goals? They're fine things in themselves, but there is something more; there is His main goal for you. He says: "I bore you on eagles' wings and brought you" — (where?) — "unto Myself."

Here is the jewel at the heart of the rock, the hidden spring, the preciousness that can be your own for the taking. If this becomes your prime goal, the shining star to which your personal wagon is attached, you can be sure that your life will be rich and that all the peripheral things (job, living situation, education, friends) will be His best; you will know fulfillment you can know in no other way.

3

A Roadmap To Utopia?

Why do you want to get married? (If you don't, you can skip this chapter.) Seriously, why? Ever thought about it?

Thought about it! I think about it every day! What's with this woman?

But what's *your* reason? There are dozens, of course: status, sex, security (both economic and emotional), strenuous social pressure, children, companionship.

Anything wrong with these?

Not really. But in view of the fact of who you are and what God envisions you becoming, maybe they're not good enough.

Toss these reasons around in your curly little mind:

1. That you can be a real helpmate to a man whose devotion to God can take him (and you) to the ends of the earth.

2. That together you and That Man can serve God better than either can separately.

3. That you might bring up children to be princes and princesses in God's family (the seed royal, if you please), and you know that's no cinch in today's drug-saturated, demon-infested world.

Is there a difference between the way a Christian and a non-Christian look, or should look, at marriage? The first motives I mentioned all come under the head of the "normal" and "natural." Now the Christian life in many ways is supranatural and takes into consideration the reality of the supernatural; therefore, it's not surprising if the Christian motives for marriage are not the same, or not *only* the same as the non-Christian. Anytime our motives aren't of a different quality than the non-Christian's, we are in danger of forgetting we're God's women living in a warped world: "God's picked representatives of the new humanity." That's what you *are* — part of a whole new race with a new life, *His* life, existing within you!

O.K. I think I've got my priorities straight; I want God's will for my life and God's man, but why hasn't he arrived? Where is he? There's been no clattering of hooves on my driveway lately and — where is he?

Honey, maybe that's part of your trouble. Are you realistic about all this? Just who are you looking for anyway: Sir Galahad crossed with James Bond, maybe? The perfect man? And if you found such a creature-from-Mars, what would you do with him? For that matter, what would he do with you? You're perfect, perhaps? And are you sure you'll recognize him when you meet him?

Of course I will!

Every woman since the beginning of time has had a built-in assurance that when her man shows up, she will, by some mysterious, intuitive process, *know!* Eve couldn't have had much trouble recognizing *her* man, in Eden, but twentieth century America is something else. Have you set a height and coloring; does he have to look like some rock star or the latest hero on TV?

Nonsense! How silly! I don't care how he looks. Of course . . . I'm 5"10½" in my nylons, so he'd better be taller than that. And he'd have to be able to support me in the style to which I intend to become accustomed. And . . . .

Hmmmm.

Funny thing. God knows not only what you are like today, but He knows what you're going to be like ten or fifteen years from now — and that you *don't* know. Furthermore, He knows what this Joe who sends your blood pressure soaring is going to be like ten or fifteen years from now and whether he'll be able to make you as happy then as now. You're really pretty safe to include God in this matter; in fact, you're *only* safe in this way.

Instead of telling God what you want, like sending in an order slip to Sears, how about asking Him to supply the man who will really be right for you, not just today, but for the woman you'll become?

Have you ever thought about praying for this man?

Have I ever thought of anything else? You haven't been listening.

No, I mean have you prayed for this unknown man's life, his growth, his problems *now?* Unless you're planning to rob the cradle, he's around somewhere, and he *needs* your prayers. You can pray as one of my young friends does:

> That he will grow into the kind of man God wants him to be; a man in the truest Biblical sense of the word — one whom I can trust as head of the home we will share.
>
> As I give him to God in prayer now, it will be easier to give him to God (and continue giving) later. If God and I are already sharing this relationship, it will not tend to be so much of a "replacement" for my relationship to God because God is already part of us.

As you pray for this man who, hopefully, is coming into your life, how about praying that God will be preparing you for being his wife? In the experiences of each day, in the difficulties which may seem quite unrelated, even in this waiting time, can you trust God to be forming you into the right girl for this particular man? If you have difficulty thinking so explicitly, do you trust God to be preparing you for marriage in general?

Just how realistic are you about marriage? Are you thinking that when your prince rides up in his white Jaguar it will be the end of the rainbow for you, the fulfillment of all your dreams, the filling in of all the hollows of your personality? If you're approaching marriage with this attitude, you're in for a bit of a shock. "Marriage is ordained of God," the ancient ceremony begins. After your relationship with the Lord, it can be one of life's most beautiful and fulfilling experiences. But when the rice and the white veil are put away, you do not suddenly emerge as a superior being. You are the same girl you always were — happier, more complete, but Cinderella you are not. You have not become (overnight), poised, serene, mature, and always lovable. Nor, fair one, has he. The first morning you wake up in his arms and realize this is your guy for the rest of your life, everything could be pink clouds and romantic music, but marriage is created; it does not just happen. It's a building together, and it takes time.

In the human arena we need one another badly, but there comes a time in even the closest human bond when each *is* an island, each is entirely alone in a situation. Do we become overwhelmed, thrown off balance, and miserable because we are not receiving the approval and attention for which we hunger? If God is our integration point and His love and total acceptance of us in Christ Jesus are feeding our hearts, we will not be asking the impossible in our horizontal relationships. We will recognize the other person's finiteness as well as our own and will let God develop us into balanced personalities. If we recognize this and let God fill the hollows in us, we will not put an intolerable weight on human relationships.

Hey! How'd we get into marriage talk like this? Remember me? I'm the gal who wants to be married but there's no man in sight.

Sorry. Just wanted you to remember that marriage is not two steps above the angelic state.

Are You Above Rubies... or Why Should He Want YOU?

Admitting the painful probabilities that statistics bring to light — that there just aren't enough men to go around — where do we go from here?

Let's be brutally honest: if you do run across this dreamboat of yours, what makes you so sure he'll fall for you? Look at your list of requirements:

1. He must be a *Christian*. That immediately narrows the field, doesn't it? What *kind* of Christian? Oh, a Strong Outstanding one. What about *your* Christian life? *Now*? Would a S. O. Christian pick you?

Oh, I'll develop and grow: together we'll become a great team. Right now I have to concentrate on other things, but after I'm

41

married, watch me.

Uh-uh. Your priorities are upside down. And besides, *you* may see your potential, but *he's* only going to see what there is to see.

Are you allowing God to make changes in your personality *now* that will be necessary in the future, or are you being unrealistic and saying, "When The Man comes, he will look below the thorny, domineering, self-centered surface and see the Real Me"? Why *should* he? There are lots of girls around whose exterior matches their interior, and why should he have to dig down to see if a gentler, sweeter you exists below that outer shell? It's God who looks at the heart, not some poor finite male.

We have only today, and as His children, His ambassadors, our first calling is in these roles. As you put Him first and develop along the lines *He* picks out for you, you begin to manifest the qualities that will attract the type of Christian man you'd like to marry. Make sense?

Next requirement:

2. *A real brain.* Seems to me two things come up here:
   a. Are you developing the brain God gave *you* so that your man will find you stimulating and interesting?
   b. Are you *over*-developing the brain God gave you so that you're becoming Miss Know-it-all and a bore? With some notable exceptions, I'm convinced that there aren't many things more upsetting to the male ego than a female super-brain. If you're blessed with an unusual set of brains, use them, won't you, to keep from showing them too much?
3. You want him *kind, gentle, understanding, romantic, tender, passionate, humorous* . . . . Yes . . . well . . . .

In the first place, how about checking up on your own qualifications in these departments? Are *you* always kind, gentle, understanding, etc.? Then, be realistic, won't you? As you have patience with your own shortcomings (few though they may be!), and as you tend to feel that these kinks will be ironed out with maturity and time, how about allowing him the same privilege? Remember that the man you meet is not a finished product. You may meet a delightful man who's been married several years; you may sigh and say, "If I could find a man like *that* . . . ." Well, he may have been fine before marriage, but he's become much of what he is through marriage. His wife has taught him many things, and being a husband and father has honed his good qualities to a fine edge, blunted sharp places, softened and refined, all of which is part of what a good marriage does for either partner. *You* will have a part in bringing out the best in your man, so don't look for perfection.

4. *He has to have many interests, be versatile, adaptable.* And you, lady? What are you doing about your interests? How much do you know about painting, sculpture, music, plays, books, sports?

Well, but until we meet, I won't know what he's interested in. When I discover that, I'll bone up like crazy.

Too late, little gal; there isn't time. And we're talking about *being.* The more you learn of these things, the more exciting life itself becomes and the more exciting person you become. By widening your scope, you can't lose — married or single.

Of course, you're not going into some kind of educational marathon or do-it-yourself-two-month-Culture-Course. But for your own sake and for the fun and excitement there is in just the doing of these things, try out a lot of things to find out what really interests you. Try a variety, but give each one a fair chance. If you think an art gallery a bit overwhelming, get an art book or two from the library and read about one artist or one particular school of painting that strikes you. Then go to your local art museum and see those paintings. No more. I think the mere word "museum" brings a glaze to the eyes of many people because they have attempted to see ALL the Smithsonian in one morning (with the National in the afternoon!) or the Metropolitan in New York between lunch and tea. One's brain becomes paralyzed. See *just* the pottery exhibit, the Indian rooms, the costumes of the First Ladies, or whatever intrigues you, and then go have a coke. Have you discovered your own local art galleries? None in Frothing Falls? Well, see if there aren't some within easy driving distance.

Read books. In the local library an enormous adventure awaits you with doors opening down many avenues. Don't just concentrate on the latest best seller which may be merely one more tour through the Penny Arcade (*any* fool can write a porno!), but get in touch with some great minds of the world who have written on an endless variety of subjects. You'll be having a great time becoming a great person, growing into the woman God wants you to be *and* becoming more interesting to the opposite sex. The other way you lose out on both levels.

You want:

5. *A very masculine man.*

And how feminine are you? Feminine, we're saying, not sexy. Your clothes, your hair-do, your walk (so few girls walk beautifully), your voice (would yours crack a goblet?), your laugh (do you bray?) — all these things have to do with femininity. What about your humor? Is it gentle, clean, clever without a cutting edge? Male egos are fragile at best; you can damage them with a cutting tongue.

Have you given thought to what you'll have to *give* this

man, or are you a gimme gal?

I like the lady in Proverbs 31, the one whose "price is above rubies." Granted that she was married and a mother, but out of a list of some twenty-four good qualities, only four or five have to do specifically with her married state. All the others which God seems to admire are available for you single girls, and surely even this lady developed a lot of her good points before her husband came charging up to her castle. So let's skip the references to hubby and kids and look at what made her so valuable.

She works willingly with her hands. Operative word: willingly. Are you working willingly at whatever your job is *now?* Ever notice how people enjoy being around someone who works cheerfully? They do good work, seem happy doing it, and the people around them are infected by their cheerfulness. We all have to work some of the time — most of us much of the time. Why not enjoy it?

She brings her food from afar. Ruby sounds like a pretty good shopper who doesn't mind chasing across town for a bargain. Are you practicing economy in your apartment with the other girls?

She rises while it is yet night. Ho HO! No breakfast in bed for this chick; she's a lady who gets on with it. Why on earth is she up so early? Perhaps to avoid the rush to the shower, or maybe she just likes the time when all is peaceful in the house so she can prepare for the shocks of the day. Staggering from the arms of Morpheus into the kitchen for a stand-up cup of coffee and then running for a bus is not a day-starter geared to inner serenity and creativity. Maybe, too, she spent time with the Lord getting her directions for the day and having Him buckle on her armor for the battle?

She considers a field and buys it. She seems to have had plenty of initiative and business acumen. Your single years can be a fine period in which to acquire skills of all sorts, among them, managing money. It's interesting that statistics show financial problems to be one of the major causes of difficulty in marriage. If you learn to handle money now, you'll have something for good vacations or for your pet projects and avoid contention later. Ruby is obviously not frittering away her hard-earned cash on nonessentials, but is shrewdly making a good investment. For those of you now in business, all this should be an encouragement.

With the fruit of her hands she plants a vineyard. Now obviously a Kansas City apartment is not the place for growing grapes, but I think we could do worse, even in cities, than to start growing our own food.

In a window box, maybe?

Why not? I wouldn't recommend cabbages, but herbs are good as a start, and what's wrong with a tomato plant? Not only will you be getting food free from dangerous chemicals, but you'll have the fun and healing inherent in working with "green things growing" and poking around in good dark earth.

She girds her loins with strength and strengthens her arms. No, I don't think this means she was an Amazon. It does sound, though, as if she were not afraid of being physically active; maybe she had a daily workout at the local YWCA. Taking good care of one's body is not only fun, but a responsibility. "Have you realized the almost incredible fact that our bodies are integral parts of Christ Himself?"

She sees her merchandise is good. Apparently, the lady was a good craftsman and took pride in her work. What a thrill to realize we can give ourselves the excitement of doing something well! Whether we are baking a pie, making out insurance policies, arranging flowers, writing letters, or cleaning the kitchen, we can do it with all the skill and creativity we can muster (and have time for!). We are told: "Whatsoever you do, do it as to the Lord."

How can we ever do shoddy work if we keep this in mind? Someone has said: Duty does some things well; love does all things beautifully. For example: you might carefully fix a tray for your sick friend; the food is hot and good. That's duty (She *is* your roommate, isn't she?). But add a lovely tray cloth, a candle, and a rose, and you have something of beauty to share. Or you find you must break an engagement with a friend, and you phone her so she will know she's free. That's what should be done, yes? But if you drive by her home, taking her a book she's interested in or one of your record albums, it adds the lustre of graciousness to duty.

Her candle goes not out by night. (Doesn't this gal ever sleep?) Perhaps she's just ready for any emergency: a sick call or people dropping by in need of a bed; maybe the candle's by the telephone just in case. Or maybe it's just an indication that she has not set time limits on her availability. We're called to "lay down our lives" for others, aren't we? And I'm sure there are times when going to the lions might seem easier than opening the door at 1 a.m. to your most UN-favorite alcoholic or junkie. This, though, is what Christian love is all about, isn't it? Time is one talent God gives us all; everyone has twenty-four hours; how do we invest our gift?

She lays her hand to the spindle in conjunction with *she makes herself coverings of tapestry:* it sounds as if she made and designed her own clothes, doesn't it? No dowdiness for her; her clothes are purple silk. If you can't make your clothes, be creative in choosing them. This also could apply to the taste and care you expend on your home. Beautiful things need not be expensive; and charming surroundings, as well as a charming appearance, speak well not just of you, but of the Lord you serve, who loves beauty.

She strengthens the hand of the poor. Well, *that's* something you can be doing without waiting for your Hero!

Our Lord says so much about the poor that we'll have trouble evading it if we're careless here. It need not be a federal project. How many things do you have hanging in your closet right now that you haven't worn for over a year? Why not share these with someone to whom they would be new, exciting, and possibly very necessary? Food, transportation, too — there are a number of tangible things one might share. But what about people you know who are poor in friendship or paupers in fun; poor in home life or impoverished in beauty? How about "strengthening their hands"?

She makes fine linen and girdles and sells them. There's that practical, good business sense coming out again. (Wonder what she does in her spare time?) This looks like a good combination of the creative and the practical. Ruby gets all the fun of making beautiful things and then doubles her pleasure by selling them. Who knows, maybe she uses the profits for her poor?

Strength and honor are her clothing. Now we already know this lady is well-dressed; purple silk and tapestry were "in" that year, so what's this strength and honor clause? Reminiscent, isn't it, of "whose adorning, let it be a calm and gentle spirit"? In neither case is the emphasis on tangible clothing, but on the adornment of the spirit. Calmness and serenity are qualities that seem to have departed with the Model-T, but they still have a compelling effect on the jaded or overstimulated of this beleaguered generation. Even if they did not, these are the qualities that are "very precious in the eyes of God."

She will rejoice in time to come. "Strong and secure in her position, she can afford to laugh, looking ahead." With God's love and guidance you can develop into this kind of woman who, married or single, is a fulfilled, whole, excitingly beautiful human being who can laugh because she knows her future is secure.

Secure? Who's secure?

Secure in the love of the Lord who never fails, who is never indifferent or too busy to talk with us. Secure in the assurance of His constant care, of His promises that He will give us everything we need, of His total understanding at all times and in all places. If you are really living in the reality of these things, *you're* secure!

I love the next: *She opens her mouth* (Most of us stop there!) *with wisdom* (How little that comes out when I open mine is wisdom!), *and in her tongue is the law of kindness.* Not just kind words, but the *law* of kindness: don't say it if there's a chance it will hurt. Even if it's true, could it hurt someone? Would I want Mary to hear me tell this laughable incident which really makes her look like a fool? If it were about me, would I want the story told? Does it build me up but make someone else look small? Questions like these show the law of kindness at work.

She eats not the bread of idleness. "Lots of free time" has been the hue and cry of Madison Avenue for years, but not knowing what to do with free time has gotten lots of people into lots of trouble. There is so much that's creative with which you can fill your time, but it takes planning. We need to have an idea-book somewhere (in the desk or in the head) for those lonely evenings, the times we feel lazy and indifferent, the days that seem dull indeed. When I was a little girl (and we won't go into how long ago that was, please!), I had a tiny set of red leather books with blank pages. One was my What-to-Do book, suggested I suspect by mother after the forty-fifth time of: "MOTHer! What can I do NOW?" In it I had listed all sorts of things I enjoyed doing. When boredom struck, I went to the little red book. If you're like me (today), you forget there's that nice pantsuit you've cut out but haven't finished, the sweater begun before hot weather set in,

49

the new cooky recipe, the friend whom you promised to call sometime. Oh, and that new exhibition at the uptown gallery — Yikes! Tonight's the last night . . . .

Enough about Ruby, but she's an exciting individual. God would not have said this much about her in His Book if He didn't think highly of her qualifications. Maybe we should do a little homework?

One further thought: Marriage involves children. Are you equipping yourself for motherhood? Rather than crying the blues over your spinsterhood, are you doing anything to prepare yourself for this role? Are you developing attitudes, opinions, and traits of character that will enable you to live your faith and also equip you for a concerned involvement with the issues which will confront your child in his school, in his social life, and later in the world of affairs? Margaret Mead, in a recent article, reaffirms the cogent point that "what is done by the individual *does* matter in the world." Your preparation involves the way you treat the individuals for whom you are *now* responsible in our sick society.

5

Hearts Are Trumps

Of one thing I'm quite sure: with many of us, God waits until we stop clutching, stop shouting at Him, stop making an idol of this marriage thing. Can you really let it go and say, "O.K. I'll leave it up to You; if You really want me to, I'm willing to accept singleness"?

Of course, of course. But I'm sure He does not want this of me. It's just not natural. I'd be happy to if He asked it of me, but He wouldn't really . . . .

He might.
Especially if you have such a tight hold on it that it's strangling your spirit. You know, when God pronounced Eve's sentence, part of it was: "Thy desire shall be to thy husband." I'm wondering if

this immense, clinging, psychological dependence on man which is part of us as women is not something we should face as part of our fallenness. You must know by now that I'm very much for men, for love and romance, but it is far too easy to be totally caught up in it. We'll jettison any plans, rearrange our lives or our hair-dos; we'll work our fingers to the first joint, throw up a promising career, and too often even undercut our best friend — all for some man we find compellingly attractive. Isn't this a misuse of one of God's greatest gifts? Moderation, balance — these are not essentially feminine characteristics; we're extremists, and that characteristic can wreck us. We need God to undertake the handling of our rampant emotional natures.

Whatever makes us think we're better than Abraham? Part of God's purpose in His great test of Abraham's faith when He asked him to sacrifice Isaac could have been to show Abraham that he was too utterly taken up with the son God had promised him and so God had to loosen his hold and free him from possessive love. It's the heart attitude that's the real touchstone, isn't it? God has to win in this area before we're ready for marriage.

For years I squirmed inwardly over that verse in Proverbs: "Give me your heart." Why was I so slow to learn that He only asks for my heart in order to protect it? How many hurts would He have saved me if I had just trusted Him? Let's think about this: Who says it? The eternal, majestic Lord of all the earth — Jesus Christ who agonized on a cross of wood, who wanted us to know God whom to know is life eternal. Can we trust Him?

"God made our hearts, and our hearts are restless until they rest in Him." Too often we live on the premise that our heart, this huge emotional part of our feminine nature, is our own to manage as we like or to give away. Our great and wise Heavenly Father will allow us to proceed on this premise if we insist. And when that heart is damaged — as it often is — He'll still heal it and bind up the wounds, but what He is asking is that we voluntarily give Him this heart *before* it gets hurt so that He can tenderly protect it.

Webster's definition of "heart" is intriguing:

- "a hollow, muscular organ" — Hollow? That means it can be filled with something.
- "the core of" — The core of *you.*
- "seat of emotion."

Can you possibly relinquish this essentially feminine part of *you?* We're willing enough to give it — gladly, no questions asked — to the man we love but dare not entrust it to the One who made it!

The Bible talks a lot about the heart. "Wherever your treasure is, you may be certain that your heart will be there, too."

How does this affect me? I don't get it.

The Bible says our hearts are tricky and wicked. That's hard to accept unless we've really faced our own rebelliousness against God, our innate insistence on autonomy, our own trickiness in rationalizing our motives and lying about them to others and to ourselves.

The real mind-blower was said by our Lord Himself: "It is from the inside, from men's hearts and minds, that evil thoughts arise." As you look at the list the Lord details, notice that among those called Big Sins that "do not concern us at all" there are several that definitely do:

Lust, theft, murder, adultery *(not my problem),*
greed, wickedness, deceit, sensuality *(well),*
envy, slander, arrogance, and folly *(Oh!).*

There are quite a few on this list that I know crop up all too often in *my* heart.

"Where your treasure is . . . ."

We pour our earnings and our savings into the things that mean a great deal to us; it may be expensive furniture and decorations for the apartment, it may be a house which really becomes our integration point, or it may be a sleek car or our wardrobe, but our hearts get very involved with that for which we've spent money. You don't think so? Think of something in which you've invested a lot of money. Then ask yourself: How much of my day do I spend with this possession or hobby; how much of my time am I thinking about it? Would I be willing to let this go if I were convinced God was asking me to? If you're honest with yourself, I think your reaction will reveal that your heart *is* involved.

So this is wrong?

Depends, doesn't it? *How* involved are you? *How* tightly are you clutching? *How* shattered would you be if you lost this treasure of yours? Can you give Him your *heart?*

My heart? But this is my area. It's me. I know what I want in the love area; God just doesn't seem to understand. He hasn't done too well for me up to now. I can't just turn it over to Him; why He might
    take away my liberty . . .
        spoil my fun . . .
            send me to Africa . . .
                make me an old maid!!

There is a place at the very center of our being that belongs to God alone, "a God-shaped vacuum in the human heart," and we force a human being, any human being, into it at our peril.

Oh, if God will just give me this one thing: if He will just bring the man into my life, then together we . . . .

"Give me your heart."

Why does He ask this? He knows the secrets of the heart; He knows this is our most precious, irreplaceable, vulnerable possession; it's us in essence. Why would He ask us to relinquish this to Him? Ah, but that's it, you see; He wants to take your heart and shield it; He wants to keep it from breaking. This is why He asks you to trust it to Him; not to deprive you, to prevent you from a great romance, (I'm convinced God can arrange a much more beautiful romance than we can ever dream up), but He knows our vulnerability in this arena where women have been losing battles for centuries. "It's the woman who pays" is the axiom drawn, not from your Sunday school teacher or preacher, but from worldly-wise people all through the years who have seen what fools we women can be.

God loves you too deeply to want to see you hurt. He's watched millions of women through thousands of years as they destroyed themselves in this area; He *made* that heart of yours, and He knows that anyone or anything besides Himself enthroned there will bring frustration and, quite possibly, despair. We'd make far fewer mistakes if we entrusted our love life to His keeping. God must shed anguished tears over us as we batter our hearts and make shipwreck of our lives in this tender area He planned to be one of the most beautiful.

"Above all that you guard, watch over your heart, for out of it is the source of life." We are all too painfully familiar with a divided heart: part of the heart for God and *this* area, clutched, held tight, for *me.* I may be quite willing to let God have His way in the areas of career, recreation, and travel, but not in my friendships. "I *must* have friends. If He does not supply the ones I think I need, and *now,* I'll supply my own. Especially men." Or I may be quite committed in friendships and quite open to God's leading in most things, but *don't touch my purse!* I work hard for my money! I know what I need! *I'll* decide how that money will be spent!

And who, in the final analysis, supplies the money? In Malachi 3:10 —

Malachi! Where's that?

Last book of the Old Testament. He asks us to prove that He will do something wonderful for us. It's a tremendous promise with a not-too-difficult condition attached. He says: "Bring ye all of the tithes into the storehouse, that there may be meat in mine house, and prove me now herewith . . . if I will not open you the windows of heaven, and pour you out a blessing, that there shall not be room enough to receive it."

If you really want to see some exciting things happen in your life, try giving Him at least ten percent of your income.

What? I can't pay all my bills on my salary now! How can I . . . .

Prove Him. If you acknowledge His Sovereignty, His right to all you have in this way, He guarantees to give beyond measure. This, to quote David Livingstone "is the word of a Gentleman of the most strict and sacred honor."

When I read, "Unite my heart to fear thy name," I get a picture of a magnet poised over steel shavings: big pieces, little pieces, some dull, some glittering, scattered like sawdust. The magnet moves over them, and they all come together and attach themselves to the magnet. Only God can integrate the shards of your personality splintered by self-will or the twentieth century ills.

Maybe yours is a fearful heart and you are afraid — afraid of loneliness, of losing out, of being single, of being unhappy. "Say to them that are of a fearful heart, be strong, fear not: behold, your God will come." No human being can allay the deep-rooted, sometimes nameless fears that may assail your heart, but He can — and He will if you will let Him. He knows, too, that hope deferred sickens your heart. There are no age limits to this malady. What's the answer? "Pour out your heart before Him." Let it come: tears, rage, the lot; pour it out. He cares about those tears, and He promises to heal the broken-hearted; His understanding *is* infinite.

"Take delight in the Lord, and He will give you the desires of your heart."

He will? Well now, this ought to be easy. All I have to do . . . .

What are the desires of your heart? Travel, a career, joy, a husband, home, children, beauty? What are the *deepest* desires?

Will He really give me all these? Any desire I have?

What about the first phrase? It says *delight,* not just believe, trust, or even know. Do you delight in Him? When God Himself begins to fill your heart, your desires pick up the reflected light from His beauty and become desires of wonder that He *can* and will fulfill.

Have you ever thought that if you permit God to work, He'll make you into just the right woman for the man He's picked out for you? How many times do we Christians miss out in our lives because we charge after something that looks like the real thing and manage to miss the extraordinary thing God was arranging!

The Waiting Game

I think many of you are showing considerably more common sense than my generation did at your age in that you do realize that there is more to life than marriage, that you are not just waiting around but are busily carving out attractive niches for yourselves and are extending your personalities in many different directions. I salute you. But others of you are just filling in time until marriage comes along.

Right here, I'd like to suggest, is Mistake Number One. Few things terrify a man more than the feeling that the girl he's dating is just waiting to pounce and lead him, a bound sacrifice, to the altar. (For some reason, known only to himself, a man seems to feel we possess some magic or carry around some mysterious potion that can lure him into a cutaway, pop a white carnation into his buttonhole, and have him moving down the aisle before he has had a chance to say, "I didn't mean *that!*"

Certainly you may want marriage; certainly it's on your mind — but not *all* the time and not with *every* man you meet or date. Men are people, and a lot of them are extremely nice to know for themselves, not just as matrimonial possibilities. Have you seriously considered other-than-romance relationships with men? They make marvelous friends once they really trust you and understand you're not sneaking up on them with a halter and bridle in hand. This may take some time and patience on your part because some have been made wary by our over-anxious sisterhood. And you must mean it; no games.

Let a good friendship ripen. If more is meant to come of this, God will let the man in on the idea, you may be sure. God doesn't say, "Now, Mary, *there's* the man who'd be exactly right for you. Come now and let us scheme together to trap him."

Pray over your relationships; not, "Give me this man!" but, "Show me how to keep my hot little hands off and let *you* bring something of beauty out of it." Accept male friendship as something richly rewarding for its own sake. Men can widen your understanding of human nature, stimulate your mind with their straight logic (as opposed to your intuition), and, ideally, bring you great spiritual richness. Get to know your brother's friends and your friends' brothers. Pray often over these contacts, asking God to keep you from impossible dreams, asking Him to show you how to keep it truly exhilarating and wholesome, asking just what *He* wants in this particular friendship at this particular time.

Note: If you're thinking of a nice, platonic friendship with some man you know who is married, forget it! Being a Christian is simply *not* a protection against being tempted. It's dangerous ground and might qualify as being the gun you didn't know was loaded. You won't lose out if you bend over backward to avoid this type of involvement. A couple as friends — great! But not just the male half, please. Even if you find yourself making too frequent trips to the pastor's study, look over your motives honestly; his wife will appreciate it.

Your life can become infinitely richer if you stop clutching. Men recognize the predatory female at fifty paces and develop the Bachelor Syndrome. Symptoms: that guarded, wary look in the eye; elaborate excuses for breaking social engagements trotted forth at the last minute; a sudden, frantic leap to the safety of men friends or married friends. But haven't we made them like this? Aided and abetted, of course, by just a bit of conceit in the male personality.

Relax, won't you? When you do meet someone great, or even fair, try thinking of him as a human being with hopes, fears, and aspirations of his own. Leave *you* out of the picture for awhile; see how he ticks. Quiet down and listen! You'll make some lasting friends this way. And friends have friends . . . .

She keeps talking about these men. I don't meet men, and I certainly don't have dates.

So you don't have dates. Why not?

Why not?

Seriously, why not? There isn't any one reason; if there were, all you girls would need to do would be to put your heads together, pool your ideas, write a book, and start cutting coupons, but what's *your* excuse?

I keep telling you: I don't meet men.

Well, it does take some males around to make dating feasible, that's for sure. And right here may be the place to bring up those uncomfortable statistics again: it's possible that where you live there really aren't many men. Less so in England, they tell me. I'm writing this part of the book on a farm in lovely Cornwall, and I'm told there are far more single men here than there are girls. I don't think it's disgraceful to consider going where there *are* men. Note: Consider. You need to be sure God wants you to make that move, and it will usually be for other reasons as well. Before a lot of you stampede for one-way tickets to the Cornish coast, consider this. If you go to farm country where there are eligible males, you're not going to snag one of those nice country lads and hustle him off to your sophisticated white-and-gold apartment in Manhattan to live *your* life. He's probably too smart to get all cooped up in a city. *You're* the one who changes locale when you marry, and are you sure you'd make a good farmer's wife?

A thought for those of you who may be treading water in a relationship with a man, going on month after month and even year after year with no commitment on his part. There are men, and I'm sorry to say that some are Christian men, who will go on indefinitely in a man-woman relationship without ever resolving it. Now that's just dandy if *you* are satisfied, but I'm thinking of those of you who carry a daily hope that one of these days he's going to ask you to marry him. It's possible he's never asked you to sleep with him, but he takes up your time, eats your good cooking, has you mending his socks and making his phone calls, cries on your shoulder now and then . . . in short, takes from you many things only a wife would give him and has no intention of ever changing your status. Lady, you're wasting time. You're out of circulation and this is going nowhere. With a sisterly smile, gently but firmly show the lad the door.

One other word of caution: if this kind of brother-sister

arrangement suits you, fine, but don't let anyone trap you with the idea that you owe this man "submission." Scripture says you are to be submissive to your own husband, but there are some these days who are trying to carry this idea into any man-woman relationship, and I think there is real danger of the man making a jolly little ego trip out of this. On a personal level, the woman is commanded to submit only to her husband, as the church does to Christ, and the man is then to love his wife as Christ loves the church. That, girls, is a different balance altogether.

In the meantime, what can you be doing to prepare yourself for:

a) marriage when it comes?
b) singleness if it stays?

Oddly enough, there doesn't seem to me to be that much difference between the kinds of preparation required. Because most of the things a single girl can be doing to make herself attractive and intriguing to the opposite sex are things which develop and expand her as a whole woman. If she is left without a man in her life, she's still miles ahead.

This whole idea of doing and/or being is something that affects the whole woman. This is your time for the development of your talents, the widening of your interests, the increasing of your skills, for travel, study, and the acquisition of God-given wisdom in the field of human relationships.

God Himself is interested in you as a *whole*. Whatever your abilities and potential, now is the time for you to develop them. God does not hand out talents haphazardly, and whatever yours is, it's both your privilege and your responsibility to use it as God directs. If your talent is music: study and develop a sure technique so you will have tools to express what you wish to communicate. Learn the literature of your instrument, go to concerts, build up a record library. If finances are your problem, many libraries have excellent facilities for listening, and in all the big cities there are many free concerts available. Watch the papers. Join a music club; they're not *all* stuffy.

Are you a painter? Get with it; you may or may not believe in art schools, but whichever route you go, you know you do have to paint and paint and paint. Go to galleries; study the art books in whatever libraries are available to you; mingle with other artists and go to university lectures. Ask God to give you new ideas in your discipline; open up your mind and put your techniques and skills at His disposal.

There's a vast field for Christians in the arts and one that is almost untrammeled. All the disciplines, music, painting, sculpture, theater, and writing, are in need of pioneers who seek a way to perform in a twentieth century manner; to show with quality work that there is an answer to the absurdity of life, to the threat of annihilation, to the mechanization of man: the message being sounded loud and clear by the non-Christian artist. There are thousands of young people today whose lives might be entirely different had the Christian artist, musician, or writer cared enough to find the "how" of communication with This-Century-people. The people who have communicated have taught destruction only too well. We need to *un*-earn the devastating label of mediocrity that's been applied, so often with truth, to any art marked "Christian" in this and the preceding century.

Luther said: "Why should the devil have all the good tunes?" Why shouldn't *we* who have the Spirit of the Living God be the innovators? Can't our God, the Creator of *all things*, in "Whom are hid all the treasures of wisdom and knowledge," give to His children something revolutionary in the arts? Does He have to be bound by the old forms? Is it possible that the reason there has been so little that is really good from our side of the fence is that we have been trying to follow the trails blazed by the non-Christians? No wonder we are having trouble. The shrill despair we hear in today's music and the starkness in much of today's art reflect the deeply rooted convictions of talented men and women that life really is absurd, mechanized, going off at last into a horror of great darkness. These people are sincere, but how can we use their ideas to communicate the positive message of Christianity, the glory of hope Christ offers to all men?

Fine, lady, but just you try it. Let's see you do a "positive" painting or "beautiful" music that's new.

Agreed; I can't. But God . . . .
Has God run out of ideas? Did He stop inspiring great music when Bach and Brahms died? Did He abrogate His creative rights with the artistic disciplines in 1900 and leave the field to the disciples of destruction? It seems to me that if we really believe our Christian tenet that we are indwelt *(indwelt!)* by the Third Person of the Trinity, we should have great hope for being able to find *new* methods of expression, to show beauty and truth in a startlingly fresh way. Hasn't our limitation been that we have tried to "figure something out" rather than spending much time alone with the Lord, asking Him to show us what new thing He wants to show us? I don't think it will come cheaply or easily; it will take genuine faith and real openness before Him; it will take *hours* of prayer and much time in His Word. If we are to present God's message to disillusioned, frenetic twentieth century people, it's going to take *His* creativity expressed in special ways. I hope that some of you in the creative fields will be challenged by the Almightiness of our Creator-God and will spend long hours before Him saying, like Jacob, "I will not

go unless you bless me . . .," until You show me how to speak out Your wonder to the contemporary mind. I believe tremendous things could happen. But I also think we need to be careful of our motives in asking such things. If we're seeking fame, if we're off on a super-ego trip, something on which to make a fortune, we'd better not even start. God does not permit us to play games. I think the key to the renaissance God may be willing to grant us is in our aching longing to present *Him* to people who have lost hope, in our desire to demonstrate His character, His righteousness, His personal reality — in short, to exhibit that the God of the Bible, the God of history-past, is also God of the twentieth century and of today's men.

Hard? No — impossible. Unless *He* does it.

But back to your personal development. Not all of you have artistic talent. Learn to do things. Travel; meet people; learn to make the most of your appearance; learn to love people — all kinds of people — not just eligible males. Do things and do them well for the great King.

Have you realized that you are often the envy of your married sisters? They see you as living unfettered lives, able to spend your money on clothes, travel, or a new car; able to expand with study while they are tied down with diapers and laundry. Either their viewpoint or yours may be an extreme, but do enjoy your freedom; develop and grow; you may never again have such an opportunity. One of the most valuable lessons the Lord can teach us is the value of *this* moment in life, *this* experience. What a tendency we have to try to live in the future; when I finish college, when I'm married, when I get the promotion, after I've been to Europe . . . . But all we have is today, and it's *this* experience, *this* sunset, *this* two-day vacation, *this* friendship that we need to treasure. Squeeze the wine of enjoyment from every minute; cultivate the beautiful quality of appreciation: of God's gifts, of others, of the intrinsic value of the *now*, however much you may stretch forward toward tomorrow.

Friendship provides a vast scope for developing the things that are important in an individual's life: loyalty, humor, unselfishness, adjustment to another personality, companionship. A young friend writes me some telling thoughts: "Companionship is certainly available outside marriage from friendship with both sexes. If one can't handle or develop friendships of a fine quality outside marriage, how can one expect to give friendship within marriage, and many say a strong friendship is vital to a strong marriage." Amen. She adds: "Of course, the most important friendship one can establish is with Jesus Christ, the only friend whose friendship will never disappoint and is always, always available." Is this real? Have you ever tried it?

In the area of your personal relationship with the Lord you have a unique opportunity for closeness with Him, for developing a total trust, for leaning more completely on His strong arm because there is no other. Your married sister might *well* envy you this! Somehow we've managed to make Paul's statement about the unmarried having more time for the Lord sound pretty dreary. That must be because we have such a dull view of God. Once our relationship has become really exciting, warm, full of love and humor (Don't you ever laugh with the Lord?), then these remarks come alive. In the times when my soul has stood on tiptoe and I've flung my arms wide in sheer excitement over His beauty, I've thought, "Don't let me lose this; if marriage would deprive me of *this* — forget it."

I would be less than honest if I said I felt that way all the time. No, even at my age the hunger for warm human closeness, the protectiveness and support of a man's love, the longing for someone to hold me close bites deep at times. But I would also be less than honest if I failed to say that I would want to be very, very sure God was directing me were I to change my status. He's made life much too beautiful and exciting as it is to want to risk anything but His best.

7

The Dating Game

Tonight you have a date and he's marvelous; he has that neat, red sports car and money seems no object. Are there ground rules?

Ground rules? I hate rules. If this female thinks I'm going to buy any rules for dating . . . .

Sorry, Wrong word. Let's be more explicit: does God have any ideas about what you'll do, good places to go, things to see, how you'll react in a clinch?

Well now, really! God interested in where I go? On a date?

He's not only interested; He's *there.* And remember we've established, haven't we, that you are very dear to Him?

Why is it so important even to

discuss something so casual, so routine for some of you, as a single date? Well, why do you date in the first place? Seems rather a dumb question, doesn't it? But sifting down to basics, along with the fun, the excitement, the social acceptability, isn't the underlying idea: "This guy seems great. Wonder if he might turn out to be *really* my kind..." And what do you mean by that, if you don't mean that maybe, after you get to know one another, you might fall in love?

And what's wrong with that?

Nothing! At least you're aware of the potential, and being so, it should have something to do with whom you date. No, I'm not saying only go out with Christian boys. (Some girls complain that some Christian fellows are harder to handle than their non-Christian dates.) I do say keep in mind that this *could* get serious in a fairly short time, and if he's not a Christian, you're headed for trouble and heartache. You *do* know that Second Corinthians 6:14 is one of the absolutes for the Christian life? No New Testament handy? Allow me: "Don't link up with unbelievers and try to work with them. What common interest can there be between goodness and evil? How can light and darkness share life together? How can there be harmony between Christ and the devil? What can a believer have in common with an unbeliever?"

Evil? The devil? Why you don't know Bill! He's the greatest! He is marvelous with his parents; he doesn't even smoke pot, hardly ever touches liquor, and he's always been wonderful to me.

Right. As I mentioned above, sometimes the non-Christians outdo our Christian boys in behavior, sad to say. But the question is not one of morality; it's one of

life. You're alive with Christ's own life, and the unbeliever is dead.

*Dead! Why he's twice as lively as any Christian I know!
He's so vital!*

Dead. In God's sight, not in mine. I was dead once, too,
and so were you. "To you, who were spiritually dead all
the time that you drifted along on the stream of this world's
ideas of living, and obeyed *its unseen ruler* (who is still
operating in those who do not respond to the truth of God),
to you Christ has given life! We all lived like that in the
past . . . being in fact under the wrath of God . . . . But
even though we were dead in our sins . . . ." This explains
why Bill or Suzy or any of your non-Christian friends may
say to you, "I don't get it" (regarding Christianity). They're
not being difficult: they *don't* get it. It takes inquiring
earnest search, yes, but it takes a direct enlivening process from God Himself as well.

Well, there it is. Think about it, won't you, and remember that God never tries to spoil your fun; He loves you.

There are some who have twisted the Christian sexual
ethic to mean one can live and sleep with a non-Christian
as long as one doesn't marry him. Better think that
one through.

For whatever they're worth, most of the thoughts for
you on sex are in the "Birds and Bees" chapter, but do
realize the way you're made, will you, and the way Bill's
made? To spend a whole evening at a drive-in, cuddled up
close, with people all around you making out, well —
you're not stone, are you? Drive-ins are rather like Bernard
Shaw's definition of marriage: "The maximum temptation
with the maximum opportunity."

Nor is it quite good sense to spend long times alone
together, and then when things start getting out of hand
to reproach the Lord with, "But I *did* pray about this. I

asked You to keep us all evening." You wouldn't really put your hand on a lighted cigarette and then pray that it wouldn't hurt?

Dancing, movies, discotheques? Please! I'd rather not get caught up in that discussion. You come from too varied backgrounds, and this is an area where I feel absolutes are not given, even though some sincere people think they are. If you're underage, the Bible says that you are to be obedient to your parents. (Get your back up? But listen: "At your age this is one of the best things you can do to show your love for the Lord.") If you are of age, these are areas, I think, where your Christian freedom comes in — freedom before the Lord. Can you take this particular place, activity, date before the Lord and stay there quietly until He gives the go-ahead or until He stops you with His gentle check? You are His, and you stand or fall in His eyes, not in mine or anyone else's.

You today, more than any preceding generation, need to think through what your own line is going to be regarding drinking (not at all new), smoking (hardly new), and turning on with drugs (your generation's special contribution). It's a lot easier to withstand the crowd if you have settled in your mind beforehand what you're going to do. (This also goes for necking, petting, etc.) Face the issues, decide on your knees before the Lord, pray with your date if he's a Christian (for him, if he's not), but don't be naive about the problems that exist.

One seventeen-year-old I know had a double dose of LSD slipped to her as a "joke," and she probably will never be entirely normal again. Another girl who had started on drugs at age ten wailed, "Why didn't somebody tell me what it would do to me?" One practical defense-action: in a big Eastern city I met a girl who went to parties carrying her own unopened Coke bottle or a thermos of coffee.

How does one think re your generation's drug culture?

What are your thoughts when two of your pop idols are casualties? Janis Joplin spoke for many of you, as did Jimi Hendrix. What did drugs do for them?

You've read enough about marijuana to feel safe in trying it out? Not stopping to ask if you've also read the opposite views, one might proffer a few ideas that would make sense mainly to Christians:

1. Your body is not your own: do you have a *right* to hazard it? Do you have a right to abdicate control of your will? Can you tie this in with the injunction we have to "bring every thought into the captivity of Christ"? And authorities seem to agree that at the very least pot vitiates all initiative.

2. It's illegal, and as a Christian you are to be a law-abiding citizen. Right?

3. By taking over the controls (God's controls by right), drugs can open the door to the demonic; and if you have not thought about that aspect of twentieth century culture, ask your non-Christian friends or pick up almost any periodical.

4. How much do you want to encourage people weaker than you in a habit which, for them, could be Step One to hell?

Can you think about nine-to-fifteen-year-old drug addicts and take all this lightly? Maybe you're just a casual pill-popper: aspirin by the fistful, sleeping pills (just the mild ones), wake-up pills, nerve pills, tranquilizers. Greater inspiration for creative work? Have you looked at Arnulf Rainer's LSD paintings?

In you — *in you* — lives the Third Person of the Trinity. Take that huge thought, girls, and go off somewhere where it's quiet and ask God to make it more real to you. It doesn't say it could or should be true; it says *He does live in you.*

Your generation thinks a great deal about issues that my generation didn't bother with until years later, more's the pity: war, civil rights, women's rights . . . . But you are enmeshed, surrounded, suffocated by an atmosphere of complete permissiveness, of everyone's doing his thing, of visceral reactions, of so-what-ness. For perhaps ninety percent of the world that you meet daily, the Christian absolutes are sold out, dead, outdated; everything is relative: you do this or that because to you it seems right at that moment. My generation often is not very helpful, I'm sorry to say. Your government is pragmatic; your courts are relativistic; your mores are permissive. Do be aware of the kind of world you face every day of your life once you leave your parental doorstep or your own apartment. Read, absorb, listen; above all, *analyse.* Listen to the lyrics of the rock music you're so turned-on by; be aware of what's being said. Lyrics used to be just lyrics; today they're philosophical statements. And please don't be unsophisticated enough to think that because the words "God" or "Jesus Christ" or "Grace" are included in some new rock song the world's getting Christianized. Nothing could be farther from the truth. Anyone who can seriously consider *Jesus Christ Superstar* a Christian statement after listening to and/or reading the words simply hasn't understood. The fact that the music is as fine as it is only adds to its subtle destructiveness.

If you see the latest destructive movie, see it with another Christian; pray before and talk about it after. Go with a group and discuss what philosophy is being portrayed here. Make no mistake; the producers of these lethal films know what they are about even if eighty percent of the viewing public hasn't a clue. If you really think about it, you'll find even in the innocuous and "entertaining" film much that, while subtly camouflaged and cleverly frosted, is sheer poison morally and ethically. We emerge subtly saturated with that philosophy which may one day erupt in some private action of our own unless we are carefully guarded.

The same goes for books. You may ask, "Why bother? Why not just avoid the whole scene?" Isn't it better to be armed, to *know* what is being thrown at you via all media, what your contemporaries and the people-who-set-the-pace are saying rather than to let it seep into your subconscious unnoticed? Do you really think you can escape it? Maybe if you burn the TV sets, never go to a restaurant where they have a radio or jukebox, never pick up a periodical (and don't think the news magazines are exceptions), never read a book, stay off buses and subways which have ads, pull down your shades, lock your door, and — suffocate — maybe then you can cut out this all-pervading attack, but I'll bet you'd *hear* something through the walls! And after all, what help would you then be to your twisted, confused, crying-out generation? Your job is to get on their wavelength. My generation has done badly on that score; too many of us are still giving you answers to questions you haven't asked. Don't make our mistakes, and *do* live your faith. Know where you're going, date-wise and otherwise.

It's naive, too, to think the former "uplifting" sort of entertainment is not scarred with this nihilism. The twisted cries and wordless struggle in much of contemporary "serious" music seeps into the mind like a miasma. The theater is saying convincingly that man is an absurd machine. The art museums run the gambit from absurdity to obscenity, the phallic symbols replacing artistic hallmarks. Some of the happenings and environments in today's art world would be hysterically funny if they were not so serious an expression of man's frenzied attempts to escape a world which to him has no meaning whatever.

Go; see and listen, but then discuss; analyse. Be aware that this is not just surrealistic madness, that behind the jarring notes and the ugliness is a real and deadly philosophy. And why not? If God *is* dead (and has it really come home to you that many people do believe this?), then what is left for man but despair?

Small word of caution: Remember I said "Pray about this." Don't go overboard and see everything going. Reading reviews on some films, plays, and books is enough to give you considerable knowledge about the contents, and there's no point in overloading one's mind with this filth. I think, too, we need to be honest before God and ourselves about our motives in seeing and reading certain films and books.

The exciting thing is that you, as a Christian, have the answer to all this. The Women's Lib movement struggles for a betterment of the status of women: fair enough. Certainly there are sincere, committed women in this movement, and some of the things they are striking out for are needed reforms. But at the other extreme there are the ones who burn the Bible with their bras (as if one were as dispensable as the other), who rant about the "vacuity of the lives of many housewives," as if the housewives were mindless robots with neither the will nor the imagination to brighten their own lives. (Getting them out to fill typing and filing jobs eight hours a day is liberation?) They also talk as if having babies were a sort of slot-machine process: the baby arrives and mother is free to walk off to work, dropping junior off at the nearest offspring supermarket without a backward glance. Mother's task, sans any joy whatever, was done the minute she came home from the hospital.

As you weigh the advantages and disadvantages of a position in this or any other movement, you may have to find yourself something less than Miss Popularity. There will be a point beyond which you cannot go and retain your Christian integrity. Seems to me there was some unpopularity among the first century Christians too.

Our Christian heritage and viewpoint are in essence different from anyone else's, and if we lose sight of this we are apt to be much less vital than the fine, moral non-Christian and be mediocre Christians to boot. (I'm speaking now of life on the horizontal, not the vertical.) A musician married to a man who doesn't understand music but is also antagonistic to it walks a tightrope trying to submerge what is for her vastly important and yet not become dis-identified. Yet she faces less of a dilemma than a Christian who tries to live her life only on the natural level with a humanist outlook and forgets that she has become, in Christ, a supernatural being with a new quality of life altogether in her veins and that this life is sustained and nourished from a supernatural source. It seems to me we have to be careful in our attempts to help in our confused and agonized society. Helping is mandatory for the Christian; she has no real choice in the matter. The question is *how?* Does she jump into the middle of one of these big activists associations where she is decidedly in the minority and where her Christian convictions are in danger of being held up to impatience and/or indifference; where she will be forced to bow to the majority; where the very methods used will often be anti-Christian in principle? Does she try desperately in such a situation to be the girl with her finger in the dyke, or does she build, with other Christians, a dyke of her own under God's direction? Does she demonstrate that God is as real and as powerful in the twentieth century as He was in the first by her whole life-style, by going about the business of helping neglected children, feeding starving people, dealing with some phase of the drug problem, giving some sense of stability to today's freaked-out kids in a way that shows her belief is not just talk? Does she live in a manner that is in itself a demonstration of personal faith in a God who still acts in the affairs and lives of contemporary man? I see the choice as one between being a foot soldier in a vast impersonal army under a leader in whom one cannot basically believe and being a vital part of a Gideon-type group with pitchers and trumpets and — God.

Science today sees man shrinking to nothing. It is learning to control killer instinct by injections. (What happens when the reverse process is tried?) It is learning how to produce babies from fetuses cradled in animal wombs and how to manipulate mentality and personality. The possibilities opened up by these and many other frontiers are chilling as well as exciting. No less an eminent scientist than Loren Eisley takes a very pessimistic view of what an expanding science is doing to man in shrinking his significance.

This isn't news; many of you, I'm sure, could fill me in on areas I've merely brushed over, but we all need to be reminded continually that we are in a real war, a battle to the death, and that's by no means an exaggeration: "For we are not fighting against people made of flesh and blood, but against persons without bodies — the evil kings of the unseen world, those mighty satanic beings and great evil princes of darkness who rule this world; and against huge numbers of wicked spirits in the spirit world."

What's all this got to do with dating?

Well, honey, the Christian is never really off-duty. Satan doesn't take any holidays, and if we think he'll observe a truce when we want to play, we'll find he's been waiting for just that unguarded moment. "So use every piece of God's armor to resist the enemy whenever he attacks, and when it is all over, you will still be standing up." Knowing your opponent, knowing it's a battle and not a carousel ride, is half the job. The other half is your enormous advantage over even the most recondite non-Christian. "You have the mind of Christ." You know where history is going; you can, if you will, be equipped with

God's power, and you can know His thoughts and live by His standards. If with all this potential you still fall down, He will pick you up.

When we actually see Christ here one day in the panoply of His glory, when every man and woman in every culture and every nation are truly under His control, aren't we going to feel humiliated and embarrassed that we didn't believe Him more fully now? This is our chance: our chance to trust Him even in our social lives and show Him whose side we're on. In heaven we'll have lost the chance to trust, you know, and — He could come tomorrow.

Whatever Became Of The Birds And The Bees ?

Maybe it's time we looked at the subject of sex.

Oh no! If there's anything I don't need it's another romanticized version of the facts of life!

Down, girl. This basic life-stuff gets us back to our original questions:

What kind of God do we have? Who are you?

This is why I think reading the book chronologically makes more sense. We've considered, in an extremely limited, ultra-finite way, what kind of God He is, and we've thought about who you are and what, under His direction, you are becoming.

Now. A quick, reflex answer here, ladies, if you please:

Does God understand twentieth century sex ethics?

In other words, has He kept up? What's His viewpoint? If you could interview Christ today, 1972: "Lord, we'd like Your viewpoint on the New Morality," what would He say?

Let's think about Eve again; she's the only one of us who ever arrived in this world in full bloom and sans the effect of fallenness. How did God design her? Well, she was female, and Adam was male, and she was to be a help "meet" (suitable in every way) for him. They were sexual beings and enjoyed all the pleasures and beauties of this unique relationship.

Let's start, then, by saying that the Bible nowhere presents sexuality, the sexual nature of man, or the sexual act as ugly or sinful in itself; it is one of God's wonders. Misused it can be the devil's own tool, but isn't this true of *any* of God's best gifts? (Is there anything worse, for instance, than a man who has a great spiritual gift and who uses it for self-aggrandizement?) So if we agree that God has made us sexual beings, and if sex, as *He* intended it, is not only good but great, can we also agree that God would have a pretty good idea of the working plan for this complex phase of our lives? A man who puts together a Swiss watch or invents any intricate machine understands better than anyone else under what conditions it runs best. Right?

Right. And since I'm not a machine, but a complex organism, and also immortal . . . .

If God does not understand our sexual nature with all its ramifications, He's not really God. If He doesn't understand today's mores and pressures, He's an outdated God, and for your purpose He *is* dead.

Is God going to have to move along a bit, read up on the Kinsey Report of *Sexual Behavior in the Human Female* through *The Sensuous Woman* and *Everything You Always Wanted to Know About Sex* and then say, "Well, now. The Revised Twentieth Century Edition of Heavenly Sex Ethics has listed the following changes . . . ."? Or is God *God* and are we still His "workmanship created in Christ Jesus," created in His image, still running best when doing so according to His blueprint for our behavior?

There's a blueprint?

We accept the Bible as God's revealed thought. Then do we take what it says about Christ's deity, atonement, and resurrection as eternal verities on which we can stake our future, but what it says about our sex lives as outmoded? Or does what He says about sex have real wisdom, love, and knowledge of His beloved (you) behind it?

What about our sexual needs as women?

Tomes have been written on the female responses, needs and drives, complete with diagrams. One of the great fallacies of our age has been to divorce this vital drive in the human being from the rest of the total person. Deep as this drive is, it is not an isolated thing, and for a woman it is so woven into her entire psyche that to separate it is to tear living fibres apart. Women, in joyfully tossing aside their clothes with their Victorian inhibitions, have considered themselves liberated, unshackled, modern, and time after time have come crashing into the stark reality of the facts of their own natures. Sleeping with a man, with its momentary ecstasy, is not enough: we want to really *belong* to him; we hunger for permanence. Christian or non-Christian, we go against the way God made our whole being at our peril. For awhile it can be exciting; it can seem like The Answer. But for all but an extremely small number of very unusual women, the End of the

Affair is sheer agony; the psychological harm done more than offsets the temporary bliss of togetherness and physical release. Few women can face the idea of sharing their man with someone else — now, a year from now, or ever.

Well now, this "two shall be one flesh" thing: that's just for the ceremony, isn't it?

When God says, "Two shall be one flesh," unpopular, old-fashioned, and quaint as this may sound to you modern girls, He is saying that something real is happening, has happened; and when you get up and put your clothes on and go home (or he does), you are *not* the same as you were. There's been real mingling of life itself, and because God intended this to be a permanent, one-for-one-for-life arrangement, you are damaged when you try to treat it as something casual — only a necessary physical release.

Many a Christian girl (and yes, I'm afraid I do mean many) goes to her wedding night, with or without a confession session, in the searing knowledge that something unique was lost along the way; and though the night may be good, it's difficult to avoid the wish that she had kept herself for just *this* man, for *this* moment.

True, but what's done is done.

Let's hasten to add there *is* forgiveness with God and His cleansing; we can confess our failures to Him and find Him not only ready, but, in Christ, *just* to forgive. However, it's rather like the boy who drove a nail in the fence for each lie he told; he found when he removed the nails that the holes were still there. The scars do remain.

Right. I'll buy God's wisdom in this matter. I will accept that He knows how He created me and understands better than I do how this machinery of my body, soul, and emo-

tions works. But what do I do to handle this constantly churned-up sex drive? It's everywhere: in music, films, books, TV. It's on every girl's lips and in every guy's eyes — and hands. Besides, there's my own hankering that doesn't need all this outside stimulation. So what do I do?

There is an old phrase, "Avoid the occasion for sin," and as a dear friend of mine once said, "We're always so careful to experiment to see if this *is* an occasion for sin!" Don't put yourself in situations where your hormones get in such an uproar that you can't hear *anything,* let alone the quiet voice of God, and then say, "Why has He made me this way?" He made you a physical being, a marvelous, responsive being called Woman, but, like the rest of His creation, you are involved in the laws that govern His universe. As you don't expect to bring a magnet up to steel shavings and have the shavings back off, don't expect to put yourself in a situation where the magnetism and power of sex become total and then pray like mad or blame God for putting you together as He has!

Practically, what does all this add up to? For one thing, stay out of the dark! Lots of parties, group activity, dates that are action-oriented — and maybe you'd better skip the drive-ins?

So that your poor date won't feel misled, discuss your convictions ahead of time. (Be sure you *have* some!) I'm assuming you're going out with someone who won't throw you down on the bed in the first five minutes and — what were you doing in that room anyway, dearie?

And what about turning the guy on? You Christian girls can be pretty thoughtless about this you know. *You* may feel it's cute to rumple his hair and nibble his ear lobes, but do you have any idea what this does to his hormones? This isn't a fortune-telling game, but your fortune's going to be settled in a hurry if you don't find out the name of the game. I sometimes wonder if Christian girls are not guilty more often than their non-Christian sisters in the cruelty and selfishness of this baiting game: get the guy really churned up, be coy, cute, and cosy, and then, when his whole being is one big Idea, turn reproachful doe eyes on him and say, "Why Joe! I'm not that kind of girl, and I certainly thought that you . . . ." Dirty pool, ladies.

There's another angle to this game of "Let's See How Far We Can Go Without Going Over The Edge" (or "Can We Reach Orgasm Without Sleeping Together?"). You keep on playing your little gambit of "I can turn off when I want to," continue to practice this with a clear conscience (if you can), but meanwhile something is happening to your own emotional and physical machinery. You know about reflexes, automatic responses, etc. Well, a girl can so condition herself to switching off as orgasm approaches or adjust to orgasm without intercourse that when the day comes that she no longer needs or wants to switch off, the old automatic pattern goes into action and — disaster. That, dear friend and switcher-offer, is rugged and can cause a deal of marital misunderstanding.

Something else: what do we say about the glory and strength of our faith if we toy with this great powerhouse of energy, this thing of beauty, wonder, and dynamite, and make ourselves just cheap playthings of momentary desire (his and ours)? We clear our consciences sometimes by "witnessing" (Heaven help us!) — talking to our unsaved date about Christianity and then throw the whole thing in his teeth on the back seat of a car. He should think you're different?

"As a man thinks . . . ." Let's be honest: doesn't a whole lot of the trouble come from our thought life? What we toy with in our minds *does* matter; it does erupt into action, and we find ourselves gasping, "But I never did *that* before!" Where did it come from? What about those little daydreams? Our own little private fantasy world? And where did we get the idea that this is going to be easy? The Christian life is pictured over and over again as a *battle;* battles are hard, sweat-producing work: weariness, pain, and blood. We've been so conditioned by our times, the mores of our contemporaries, that we accept as "normal," as our "right," that which is out-and-out revolt against the laws of God. We are saying, "How can He be so cruel as to deny me? He doesn't really understand." May I suggest very, very gently and with great reverence that when the writer of the Epistle to the Hebrews says that Christ was tempted in *all* points as we are (yet, of course, without sin), it means *all* points. Do you really think He doesn't understand this problem?

Now aside from the activity bit and staying out of dark corners, what else? Nature still abhors a vacuum, and it's pretty hard to forget anything as potent and fascinating as sex by saying, "I won't think about it — *I* won't *think* about it." One has to think about *something,* and it had better be pretty interesting, not to say absorbing, if it's going to compete. Right? How about planning interesting active dates: golf, spectator sports, swimming, all kinds of outdoor activities, or concerts, plays, lectures, sightseeing. Share with other people, all sorts of sharing: visiting, double-dating, group-dos, doing something for people of any age who are less fortunate than you. Develop constructive hobbies together. The secret is planning, isn't it? Daniel, a vigorous young man, "purposed in his heart that he would not defile himself."

Developing real interests on your own helps too: hobbies you really enjoy, studying things that intrigue you, getting *involved.* See to it that you do all you can to avoid lonely evenings, even when dateless. Furnish your mind with as much beauty and variety as you can; you're not just a body, even though today's art, entertainment, and media all conspire to make you just that. Respect yourself as a *whole* woman: God does. He made your body with its beauty, its appeal, and its needs, but He also values your intelligence and creativity, your individuality and personality.

In the midst of your derisive hoots at the old cold-shower-and-volleyball routine (and I understand your reaction), you might just consider that stringent, enjoyable (note the word) exercise is great for the figure, for health, and you do meet some awfully nice men on golf courses, at tennis matches, skating, skiing, and swimming. You have an office job in the city? Walk, lady, walk; run, if necessary, but beauty and health are blood sisters, and beauty's never been much of a handicap in the dating and mating game.

How then does God look at sex? Obviously not as something just as an end in itself. "You cannot say that our physical body was made for sexual promiscuity; it was made for God. And God is the answer to our deepest longing." This is God speaking to you in love because He never forgets for one moment who you are. Sex is meant as the outward expression of a deep spiritual and emotional *unity,* the ultimate in expressing the inexpressible between two people made in God's image — two people who feel so deeply about each other that they want each other for life. It's like God to give us something so beautiful, so intense to express love that goes deeper than words.

Now I would be both naive and dishonest to say that there is no temporary pleasure to be had just from the sex act itself, without the permanence; the Bible does not wink at the fact that sin can be fun; it speaks of the "pleasures of sin." What I am saying is that: A) God, knowing the tremendous potency of sex in the human beings He made, intended its natural climate to be one of permanence; it is an integrated and wonderful *part* of the whole complicated structure of the man-woman relationship. It is no more a thing in itself than a beautiful Gothic doorway or rose window is the whole of a great cathedral. Actually something so explosive and so totally involving needs permanence to contain it! B) You are sadly mistaken if you think you can play with this great dynamo and walk off untouched; your whole psychological make-up makes that impossible.

But she doesn't know me. I'm different: I'm not like her....

Add that to your list of blessings, but if you're saying that you can play with matches and not get burned, — just remember — a woman is a woman is a woman, and something happens deep within her psychological make-up when she gives herself to a man. Maybe it's involved with the maternal, life-bearing role she is geared to assume; whatever it is, I do know the emancipated girl of the seventies is finding out what women have been finding out since hanky-panky began: the price is very, very high. And not in pregnancies alone is the price high, though the number of illegitimate births does not seem to be declining much, pill or no pill, and the lingering psychological anguish of abortion is the chapter they don't let you read ahead of time. No, it's the emotional shredding and tearing that comes in going from one bed to another in a rootless world, in seeing one's individuality and sense of personal value disappear, in having one's body become a "thing" to be discarded when a more exciting partner comes along. The law of diminishing returns fits here too: making out more and more and enjoying it less and less. In talking just recently to a young fellow who moved among typical American young people, I was told, "I've never met a girl who had tried sleeping around who really felt good about it," and he was speaking in a non-Christian context.

O.K. But I do love my man, and we are going to be married. You can't mean anything so lavender-and-old-lacey as waiting till the words are said? What's a ceremony?

Well, friend, there's the time and place element, for one thing. Proficiency in the sex act, even between two people in love, is an acquired, not an instinctual skill, and furtive meetings in awkward places are not really conducive to furthering this. Besides, the initial experiences for the girl are often awkward, incomplete, and uncomfortable — meaning it can hurt like crazy — and the liberated viewpoint has little to do with this; it's physical. She may need much patience, tenderness, and understanding, and any sense of guilt or urgency could not only detract but get this aspect of your relationship off to a very bad start.

Again, I'm talking to you as Christian girls to whom the living Holy Spirit is a reality. "Have you forgotten that your body *is* (not should be) the temple of the Holy Spirit, who lives in you and is God's gift to you, and that you are not (Listening? *Not*) the owner of your own body? You have been bought, and at what a price! *Therefore* bring glory to God in your body." That's the positive side of things.

A few secret meetings, some *in*-expertise on the Q.T. (and the pill doesn't always work, whatever you've been told). Is it really worth it? Are you *that* much of a slave, you who think you don't like the idea of "You are not your own"? Which is freedom: being the love-slave of the Lord Jesus Christ who went through physical, mental, and spiritual anguish beyond your wildest imaginings to buy you back from Satan's camp, or being slave to a human being's sex drives — yours and/or his? Aside from the practical aspect of the pill and other contraceptives failing to work, have you thought that just possibly this engagement of yours could break up? It *isn't* the same as marriage: the whole idea of engagements is a getting-acquainted period (and not all *that* well acquainted). Christian marriage is for keeps. Many girls have been engaged two or even three times. Sex with each man? Isn't that just a little like promiscuity?

But we'll never break up; I know we won't.

Let's hope you won't if he's God's man for you. But the pre-wedding pregnancy always causes some heartache, and there is real beauty in God's order. And let's be honest: life itself is uncertain.

We come back to the same thing: God loves you; He values you as an individual, as a whole being, as a woman. He wants to keep you from anguish; He is *not* trying to spoil your fun or make you a misfit in today's society. He knows what makes you tick, and He wants for you, each one of you, the very best.

Honest.

The Skeleton In The Wardrobe

It seems I am getting in deeper than I intended when I started all this. I thought I'd mention sex and discuss its effect on our lives and the Bible's attitude to some phases of it, but having gotten started on this subject, I'm wondering if, in all fairness to you, I shouldn't go into a touchy area that most Christian books seem to tiptoe around lightly (and apologies to any that don't).

All right, then: sex before marriage is not condoned; this is one of the Christian absolutes. But you're a physical being and you just don't know how to handle the physical You all the time. If you are assaulted by a great wave of physical desire in the middle of the night, for instance . . . .

Don't tell me to get up and

start a volleyball game. What about masturbation?

Here I may bring down on my head the wrath of many fine Christians when I say that, as far as I have ever been able to ascertain, this specific thing is nowhere explicitly prohibited in the Scriptures. So let's look the subject squarely in the eye and see what we can find.

Most of you are aware, I am sure, that the current experts in the field of relativistic sex research, as well as some totally relativistic authors of do-it-yourself manuals, iterate and reiterate with dreary repetitiveness that it is entirely a harmless practice; idiocy does not result, masturbators do not become degenerates. Still, most of us find ourselves shrinking back a little here. When we read of one avant-garde writer who sits in a cell somewhere and masturbates, we feel a bit sick.

While this practice can release physical tension and does not, if practiced alone, involve anyone else, it is a form of hedonistic self-love. It can also set loose, rationalize how we may, some plain and fancy guilt feelings. It can increase in frequency, and there might well be a point-of-no-return or how-far-can-this-take-you? Then there is the question of the fantasies that always go along with it. Because this is not sex as God intended it to be, it is a lot *less* than sex should be. Whether one gets a reaction from just the thought processes (which says a lot, by the way, about the power of thinking) or is involved in a much more physical participation, there would seem to be at least four dangers.

1) The automatic "switch-off" we discussed in the preceding chapter. Contrary to the opinion of those who advocate masturbation as a sort of warm-up preliminary to the main event, it is possible that one could get so conditioned to one's own little reflex patterns that in the marriage relationship it would be difficult to respond naturally. That nice young husband just might not come up to some of the more exciting fantasies.

2) The fantasizing could get pretty ugly, and God is the One who says, "As a man thinks so *is* he." It will become a descending spiral: wilder fantasies needed for orgasm — and what about what the Bible has to say about our minds? If our fantasies involve a particular individual, what about Christ's statement that lusting after someone by looking is tantamount to adultery?
3) The shy girl could easily use this as a further withdrawal from reality or from any one-to-one relationship.
4) There could be a spillover into "real life": the fantasy of one's own room under certain conditions could lead to saying "yes" when we meant to say "no."

Don't forget, either, the tremendous subterranean power of the subconscious; you've studied a great deal about it; it's real. We cannot control it, but we *are* responsible for what we allow our conscious mind to play with; it is this that sifts things down into the subconscious. "Fix your thoughts on what is true and good and right. Think about things that are pure and lovely and on the fine good things in others." This has been called God's prescription for feeding the subconscious.

The whole area of mechanical devices for masturbation is opening up more and more. Some cultures have long made all sorts of devices freely available; until recently ours has frowned on these, and availability was limited to under the table, dark corner transactions. Now, however, with masturbation appearing in films and being considered an indoor sport, there is a growing freedom in obtaining devices. How does all this tie in with what we know about the glory of our God to whom we are intimately related, to the fact that your body (*your* body) is part of the living Christ, the temple of the Holy? Can we seriously contemplate a planned practice of masturbation in the face of all that into which God has brought us? We *are* a heavenly people. How, then, will He implement this in this problem of masturbation?

Self-love, loneliness, frustration, physical desire — these can all be strong motivations for the practice of masturbation, but God wants something better for His cherished ones. Let's be honest with ourselves: the sex drive in a purely physical sense is not exactly the same problem for us that it is for men, and for most women it is less intense. A real urge is there, a strong one, but it is tied in with our great emotional and psychological need: we desperately need to be loved. If we really are taking in God's love for us, the reality of His nearness and our preciousness to Him, it can do a lot toward helping us cope. Can He show us how to channel the very drives He has given us?

Some practical suggestions: Notice when and where the inclination occurs and do something ahead of time. If it's an awakening pastime, set your alarm across the room, have the coffee percolator plugged in, turn on the TV, and head for the shower! Remember, just fighting down destructive thoughts gets us nowhere; these have to be *replaced*. If this thing hits in the middle of the night or as you drift off to sleep, have enough bedside distractions arranged so that you can go into action the instant you know this is going to be one of those nights. Battle stations! Turn on the light, switch on the radio, have an absorbing book handy — and why not some food? Or if activity is called for, make cookies, cut out a dress, or paint a picture. Why not? Lots of creative people do their best work in the wee small hours. Channel this drive.

Find out what things contribute to your difficulty. Bedtime is probably not the time for a sexy novel or even a how-to marriage manual. Pray, certainly, but pray *before* you find yourself drifting into the fantasy world; once that starts it's already late in the day. A clear decision made ahead of time before the Lord helps. Commit your will and your imagination to the loving Lord who really does understand, but do be practical! God has given us frightening power in our minds, and the imagination is a team of spirited horses that can drag the will behind like a chariot with square wheels.

Try reading a psalm just before turning out the light. Let God's Word be the thing that seals your mind and sifts down into the subconscious as you go to sleep. "God teaches His loved ones as they sleep."

If you are presently caught in this habit: DON'T PANIC! You may not find you can discuss this with mother, dad, or Aunt Minnie, but you *can* discuss it with your loving Lord — a Lord who *is* able to deliver.

Also, there may be some understanding person with whom you can talk. One wise statement I heard on this subject came from an outstanding leader who knows this generation of young people as few do. He said, "I never tell anyone to practice masturbation, but I do say to them, 'If you do, the Lord will forgive you as He will for other things.'"

This is not a problem that you are in all alone; many people suffer with it — many more than need to because it's been so hush-hush that people have not known where to turn for help. One might admit to fornication, to adultery, even to homosexuality, but masturbation?

In practicing masturbation you may find some consolation and release, but I think you'll like yourself better in the bright light of day if you've won through with God's help. Don't be discouraged: if you find you've been succumbing four or five times a week and reduce it to one or two, rejoice! This is progress. Rome, I've heard somewhere, wasn't built in a day, and God does know our weaknesses and will continue to aid. He may not wave a wand and deliver us instantly from every vestige of our habits; often there are trials and some heartbreaking failures — one step forward and two backward — but our God *is* a God of victory, and He is concerned in *all* that enslaves you. He wants you to be a truly emancipated woman.

Comfort, Conformity, or Camouflage?

It was a man who pointed out to me: "A man may fall in love with a woman because of her brains, her sense of humor, or her personality, but make no mistake: what hits him *first* is always her appearance." How's yours? What does it say about you? What's the Christian girl's line here? Need she suffer by comparison with her non-Christian competition? Eyes, hair, skin, figure — these are all God's gift to you and to the men in the world. (Remember the lady in Proverbs?)

Let's take clothes: great subject! All women love clothes. How about you; do you dress to attract or seduce?

Seduce! How can you say that!

Stop shouting and think a bit.

Your skirts, for instance. Are they the shortest in the whole school or office? Are you wearing hot pants to work? Exactly what are you trying to do? It *can't* be that you don't know what turns men on? In this day and age? If your dress is as tight around your derriere as it's possible to be without splitting and the front of your blouse is cut nearly to your navel, don't be surprised when the office lecher or the messenger boy finds his hands out of control. You're advertising goods you don't want to deliver, and at a pretty cheap rate, I'm afraid.

On the other hand, dresses that look as if they are designed by Omar the Tentmaker in some depressing dishwater gray or mud brown have little to do with the God who made the glorious colors all over His world and who obviously loves beauty. Think of the colors in flowers, shells, water, and sunsets; of His delight in textures and fascinating shapes; of His care in the exquisite design of the snowflake that exists for only a few moments as it drifts down and then becomes part of a vast white mass. For His own delight He causes rain in places "where no man is," making plants to grow that no one sees but Himself.

Are your clothes fun and attractive or are they your whole life? If the latter, you may find this becomes a big point of contention in marriage, budget-wise for instance. Or let's say you're very much in the hip picture. (Some of the hip clothes are feminine and graceful; these aren't the ones I have in mind.) Are you sure you're just registering protest against bourgeois conformity, or are you hiding behind all that half-clean drapery to obscure who you are? If you're really so important to the God of all the earth, why try to be submerged? You are important; you are an individual; you *matter*, girl. Dress the part.

Too often the bizarre, the tattered, the attic-y look in clothes seems to be an escape, a cover-up, an overall mask to hide behind because you don't know who you are in a hostile world. I've watched you as you come to L'Abri, shattered by drugs, by misunderstanding from my contemporaries, with psychological hang-ups, brushed with the occult, gradually coming into the sunlight of knowing who you are; in the words of one of my Malaysian "children," of knowing "I am not a machine but a human being, and very significant to Him, and I am in the image (of God) and made to love Him."

As this knowledge begins to permeate, you emerge from under the huge dull hats, the beautiful hair gets pushed out of the eyes, tentlike coverings that hide every line of your femininity begin to be replaced, and you are able to let the world see you as you are.

I'm aware that here I may be addressing at least two extremes: those of you who are in flagrant rebellion, who are shouting, "Christian freedom!" and those who, like myself, come from conservative backgrounds which tend to equate spirituality with plainness or even dowdiness. Should you want to attract indiscriminate attention just so you're noticed? Aren't we to "adorn the doctrine of God in all things"? Either extreme — flashiness or drabness — can call attention to you and says something about you. People stare and notice and point, and yes, I am talking about dull clothes as well as the opposite extreme. On one hand the danger is spiritual smugness, on the other great pride. Neither is for the glory of the Lord.

To be appealing, to be attractive, and, above all, to be feminine — this is as God made us. Have you ever thought of being feminine — in attire, voice, manner — for *Him*?

He'd really be interested?

If He made you a woman, doesn't He want you to epitomize the best that that term implies? The Bible is full of references to beautiful dress in a good sense, and beautiful raiment is used as a picture of the very righteousness of Christ in which He plans to adorn us. Over and over He speaks of beauty in clothing: "Raiment of needlework before the King"; "I decked you with embroidered robes, I shod you with Egyptian leather, I swathed you in fine linen, I clothed you in silk, I adorned you with finery, bracelets on your arms, a necklace around your throat . . . earrings in your ears and a lovely crown on your head. You were adorned with silver and gold, robed in fine linen and silk and embroidered robes . . . you blossomed into a great beauty." "Ointment and perfume rejoice the heart." "His eye sees every precious thing."

God's world is still lovely in spite of the Fall; it's filled with His own love of beauty. Remember the splendor of the priests' clothes? They had lovely colors, beautiful embroidery, even bells. Did God love beauty then only to hate it now? It's difficult to conceive of God's using beautiful things both in fact and in illustration if He disapproved their use.

Well, what's to be my guideline?

A wise Christian I once knew said he felt God's way was for a woman to dress according to her station in life. A bit quaint? Well, doesn't this give us freedom, and doesn't it mean that a pair of jeans, for instance, would be fine on the farm, in the kitchen, hitchhiking — just lots of places — but would hardly be appropriate in the White House drawing room if you happened to be invited for tea. There's something here, too, that involves compassion and concern for others; *we* have to look at you, you know! I like *Phillips* on First Timothy 2:9 and First Peter 3:3: "The adornment of a Christian woman is not a matter of an elaborate coiffure, expensive clothes or valuable jewelry . . . . Your beauty should not be *dependent* on . . . the wearing of jewelry or fine clothes." The *positive* emphasis is on that which should be outstanding about us as Christian women: the unfading loveliness of a calm and serene spirit.

Any woman knows clothes affect her bearing, her manner, her actions; we're hams enough to act up, or down, to the way we dress. You can lure men with clothes, all right, but you're apt to get exactly what your appearance makes a bid for. Don't yell, "Foul!" when some guy plunges his hand down your plunging neckline — and, honey, why did you leave your bra at home, hmmm?

But I only feel at home in blue jeans.

If you're dressed like an Appealing, Feminine Creature, the chances are that you'll act like an A.F.C. An attractive girl here wrote me: "I should always like to have fresh clean hair, a pretty dress, and favorite perfume, and more, to always be gracious, to speak gently, to listen with affection, to walk tall. I've never thought of being feminine for His sake before. It's so beautiful. And this is the real beginning of His answer to something I've asked Him to teach me about: 1) What it means and why it is so important to be related first to Him and then to someone special, besides the (dare I say it?) run-of-the-mill 'spiritual' reasons, and 2) what really is the meaning and role of a woman in an age of fragmented absolutes, uni-sex, career girls, Women's Liberation Front . . . and men who are for the most part equally unsure about their masculine role. (Help!)"

If we're really daughters of the Great King, let's dress the part: with good taste and style when the occasion calls for it, with casualness and freedom when it fits, but never afraid to be the woman God made and never feeling sex is all you have to draw to you the man you want. For the girl who doesn't know her heritage, sex *is* the common denominator; but for you who've discovered your identity in Christ, it is only part of all you are.

I am concerned over the extremes of drabness and sloppiness I see in some of you. Not from reasons like "No young lady dressed that way in My Day," or "What will the neighbors think?" but because of what it says about what you think about *you*. When I see an intelligent girl with stringy, unwashed hair, wearing baggy clothes (perhaps also unwashed), I see a girl with no confidence in herself as a woman. Your past mistakes, parents' negative view of you, what today's society is saying about Christian values, the emphasis on unisex — any or all of these may be contributing factors in making you doubt that there is anything intrinsically valuable in being a woman. If you feel you are only a sex object, a toy for the men in the world, your clothes will proclaim this viewpoint. If you feel worthless, unattractive, and unfeminine, your careless anonymous clothes will advertise this fact.

Do give some thought, won't you, some deep thought to the real *why* of the way you dress, whatever that way is. Be *glad* you're feminine; be proud to be a woman; gladden the heart of your liege-Lord. "Be beautiful inside (too!) in your hearts with the lasting charm of a gentle and quiet spirit which is so precious to God," and as part of your femininity, let your clothes say the right thing about you.

What's Your Reality Quotient?

We're trying to be realistic, right? Some of you won't get married. Only God can show you what He wants for your life, and there are some of you who will be happier single if you will just let Him point the way. (I did say *some* of you.)

Are you really sure you're cut out for double harness? There are those, you know, who aren't. Some of you are aware of this and always have been; with some it takes time to discover it, and for others the discovery comes tragically late in the day when there is no going back. One wonders how many unhappy marriages there are; how many broken ones that never should have happened at all but did because well-meaning relatives and friends put so much pressure on the girl that

105

she finally opted for anyone who could put an end to this intolerable situation. Social pressure is tremendous, and a single woman can be made to feel quite definitely that she hasn't "made it." (This may be shifting somewhat under the impact of Women's Lib.)

But if you're still honing after marriage, remember there *is* a loss of personal freedom (the two of you do merge into one) and there are some of you who would find this difficult to accept. You have an interesting career going: would you be content *if* marriage meant relinquishing this? What about all that travel you've had such fun doing or dreaming about? The restriction on your independence may become a bigger issue than you think. Even non-Christian women these days are screaming about their loss of identity in marriage and their objections to being tied down. *Your* restrictions are in a sense greater if you carefully consider the implications of First Corinthians 7:4 and Titus 2:5: even your body is no longer entirely your own. Can you live with this? Are you really prepared for these commands? They *are* commands, aren't they? How do you react to the word "obedient"? Hackles up? Watch it, lady; that's part of the Christian marriage contract, old-fashioned as it may sound.

Some of you are strongly independent by nature, really dominating personalities. A woman-dominated marriage is not a good marriage, nor is it truly Christian. Some of you, too, have been much used of God in personal counseling, in working with problem people. Be sure you go over this carefully with the Lord because, you know, it's a *rare* male who welcomes an invasion of his privacy; and although as a single you can bring people home at all hours, talk until 4 a.m., and stash them on the floor of the living room or under the sofa, friend husband, even though a dedicated Christian man, may react with Queen Victoria's classic phrase, "We are not amused."

Keep in mind, too, that you may lose a great deal of

your individuality in marriage. Whereas now you are Dawn Radcliffe, singer, painter, or decorator, with a smart identity of your own, a sleek apartment, terribly chic clothes, and opinions people listen to, you may find yourself simply Mrs. Joseph Jones, "that brilliant Joe's wife," and wonder whatever became of *ME*? Naturally, this will depend on where you live, what social group you will move in, and what Joe's like. It certainly is not necessarily true that you will be relegated to the kitchen for formula talk with the girls; you may be in a most stimulating circle intellectually, but do know what you're getting into. This isn't a job you can resign from, is it? Maybe the main reason you are discontented now is that you're struggling mentally to fit yourself into a role for which you were never intended. Ever watch a little child doing a jigsaw puzzle? He finds a piece shaped something like the hole that needs filling; he puts this piece over the space, which any adult can see isn't the right one, and he jabs and forces, trying to *make* it fit the hole. Are you trying to tell God which slot you fit?

And another thing: how ready are you for the responsibilities, the strains and stresses, the possible deprivations, the selflessness that Christian marriage demands? Women's Lib aside, have you read Ephesians 5 lately?

Be sure it's *marriage* you're reaching for and not some romanticized ideal of same.

If you're considering marrying someone, think about this: on what basis does this man get his guidance from the Lord? So many young people are satisfied when the partner-to-be is "just" a Christian. A Christian he must be, granted; but if you are a girl who has matured in the Lord, have you considered what would be involved in submitting to a baby in the faith? This could be a deep frustration for you. Yes, he may grow, but how do you know how much or how fast? You are going to have your whole life shaped by his decisions; how does he let God show him what those decisions are to be? Is he someone whose life before God is such that you can safely trust his judgment for yourself and your children?

But I don't want . . . .

Ah.
You don't want? The clay talking to the Potter? Remember the laughable but deadly accurate picture, the scene at the potter's in Romans where Paul depicts the clay as saying, "Why have you made me this way? I don't *want* to be a squat, thick pot to hold umbrellas! I want to be a tall, slender vase; *she* gets to hold flowers!"

You are His: rare, individual, precious, with a place all your own in His thoughts, in His heart. He places you "as it has pleased . . ." — whom? You? You're not wise enough, nor am I, nor is anyone. "As it has pleased *Him.*"

The thought occurs that there will be some of you who will be looking at this from quite another angle. You are deeply dedicated to God and feel He does not want you to be married — ever; that you are to make this sacrifice for Him. I would move carefully here; no one must ever be the "Voice of the Lord" to anyone else, but, especially if you are very young, do be sure it's your Father's voice you're listening to and not some masochistic urge, some lack of assurance that you can get a man interested in you, or some fear of marriage itself. God knows what He wants for you, and to be a joyful wife and mother is in His plan for most women. Only He knows if you can deny yourself this and remain free, untense, and gracious. Don't limit God here either.

Well, I've been reading First Corinthians 7 and . . . .

Yes, there *is* that passage. Where does this fit in our discussion? Some have used this as if it were *all* Paul had to say about marriage; some, who love the Lord, have had their consciences bound, feeling marriage would be a betrayal of their consecration. Each of us must always be clear before our God that we are in *His* place for us and no other. We need to take this passage in connection with all other statements about marriage that are given, not only in Paul's writings but in the rest of the Word as well. From the beginning God made man and woman, and He made them for each other; down through the years marriage has been a God-given ordinance. Christ attended a wedding and contributed to the festivity. He spoke quite a few times about marriage and its responsibilities; He used it in parables. To say Paul was against marriage per se is to ignore the things he says in Ephesians (comparing it explicitly to the relationship of Christ and the church) and what he says in Colossians and First Timothy 5. Interestingly enough, it is Paul who speaks about the degenerate last days when apostate teachers forbid people to marry. I don't think we can ignore the fact that Paul says more *for* marriage, even in the seventh chapter of First Corinthians, than he does against it. We need to keep in mind Peter's warning about taking *no* Scripture by itself.

Right. Then what is he saying?

May I quote at some length from *The Living Bible?*

Here is the problem: we Christians are facing great dangers to our lives at present. In times like these I think it is best for a person to remain unmarried. Of course, if you already are married, don't separate because of this. But if you aren't, don't rush into it at this time. But if you men decide to go ahead anyway and get married now, it is all right; and if a girl gets married in times like these, it is no sin. However, marriage will bring extra problems that I wish you didn't have to face right now. The important thing to remember is that our remaining time is very short, [and so are our opportunities for doing the Lord's work]. For that reason those who have wives should stay as free as possible for the Lord; happiness or sadness or wealth should not keep anyone from doing God's work. Those in frequent contact with the exciting things the world offers should make good use of their opportunities without stopping to enjoy them; for the world in its present form will soon be gone. In all you do, I want you to be free from worry. An unmarried man can spend his time doing the Lord's work and thinking how to please Him. But a married man can't do that so well; he has to think about his earthly responsibilities and how to please his wife. His interests are divided. It is the same with a girl who marries. She faces the same problem. A girl who is not married is anxious to please the Lord in all she is and does. But a married woman must consider other things such as housekeeping and the likes and dislikes of her husband. I am saying this to help you, not to try to keep you from marrying. I want you to do whatever will help you serve the Lord best, with as few other things as possible to distract your attention from him. But if anyone feels he ought to marry because he has trouble controlling his passions, it is all right, it is not a sin; let him marry. But if a man has the willpower not to marry and decides that he doesn't need to and won't, he has made a wise decision. So the person who marries does well, and the person who doesn't marry does even better.

Well now. Where do we go from here?

Anyone who has hung with me this far knows I am neither theologian nor savant, but it seems to me that Paul is writing to people in rather dire straits: they could be hauled off to the Roman amphitheater at any minute and tossed to the lions for lunch. He mentions "these times," "the time is short," and so on; they lived on the lid of a volcano. Certainly if today we're in a position of uncertainty (and many Christians are: those behind the iron and bamboo curtains, for instance), marriage can well be a risk. Isn't the key phrase: "I want you to do whatever will help you serve the Lord best"? In marriage one *does* have to consider the husband's likes and dislikes; there are mundane tasks to do.

What about suffering in the Christian life? Not a comfortable thought, is it? If this choice of singleness is costly — and let's face it, it is — what is our precedent? The Lord Himself chose singleness and denied Himself the comfort and solace of home and family, and if He calls us to the single life (if *He* does), we are called to a special and beautiful fellowship with Himself. If you can choose this and really not burn up with unsatisfied desire (physical, but also emotional), if you really can concentrate on serving the Lord and pleasing Him, then this special life of self-denial may well be that to which God is calling you. But don't let's hide behind First Corinthians 7 and then grumble at our lot, getting all tense, irritable, and frustrated.

If God leads us to the single life for *His* work, then we can and will live singly with joy and freedom. If we're single and *not* free about it, then either this is not His way for us or our attitude needs some revamping.

It comes to this: God created you, loves you, and *guarantees* you a happy, fulfilled life if (and the condition is all-inclusive) *if* you will turn that life over, in all departments, to Him. "I am come that they might have life . . . more abundantly." It's His *promise.*

It's that simple. And, considering how self-willed we are, that hard.

12

Mixed-up, Hung-up, or Tuned-up ?

So you find you're weak or dominating, too fat, too thin, plain, shy, loud, or clumsy. You don't have to *stay* that way. God not only loves you; He's *in* you. And He has no idea of your being the same person five years from now (or even one year from now) — unless you keep shoving spanners into the machinery. You can be the girl on the bicycle struggling desperately to pedal up a steep hill, even getting off to walk and pushing the stupid thing —

Or —

You can hitch a handhold on a passing ten-ton-truck and — GO!

"The exceeding greatness of . . . ." Whose power? Yours? You don't have any. *His*. It is available to you or God is a liar. Use it; let Him show you. All the how-to and do-it-yourself manuals on earth can only give you a few generalities, some suggestions, ideas, plans, but the Lord Almighty, the Sovereign of all the earth is your Heavenly Father. With some willing cooperation from you, He can work wonders. He knows you so well: your tastes, your needs; He put you together. He not only knows what makes you tick, but He also put the tick there. He can unlock your frozen-in personality; He can deliver you from old fears; He can help you to fullness of life. But —

There's always a but!

But you must give Him the key. Just as He does not force Himself into anyone's life in the matter of salvation but says anyone may come, He will not force Himself into your life but will wait until you open the door.

Perhaps you need help; most of us do at one time or another. He'll lead you to the right teacher, employer, or advisor. Only *He* must do the directing; don't snatch the wheel out of His hand and then blame Him for wrecking the car.

You say you're shy, can't talk? You can listen; anyone can listen. Half the psychiatrist's couches in the world would be empty if there were more loving ears available.

How can one conquer shyness, aggressiveness, selfishness, immaturity? If there are hang-ups in your personality that repel others, will God change these? Can He? He wants the best for you, lady, but it involves trust. "He could do no mighty works there." Why? You know why. Because of their unbelief.

Think seriously about your shyness being a form of conceit, will you? I was thunderstruck the day this was said to me, but gradually the truth dawned: that my shyness came from thinking about *me*: Suppose *I* fail? What will they think of *me*? How do *I* look? Will they be impressed by *my* ideas?

And that old devil: depression — the crawly blanket of anxiety that covers as we swim up to consciousness in the morning — the unreasoning, unreasonable sort of fear that slinks in from nowhere. How do we handle this? (Jesus knew depression, though from an infinitely greater reason: "He was horror stricken and deeply depressed" in the garden.) There are a good many practical things to do; seeing a good doctor would top the list if it persists. Sometimes extended treatment might be indicated, but get it. There are medications that a doctor might prescribe that could assist. If you're finding this sort of thing clouding your mind and knotting your stomach, try:

— confession at night; going over your whole day and bringing your failures under the blood of Christ. Shouldn't we do this in any case?
— reading His Word last thing, even if only a short portion.
— praising Him immediately upon waking.
— committing yourself and your day to Him.

And do memorize some verses; it is warm and sustaining to be told in the middle of a lonely night when there is no one to care, no "feeling of belongingness" anywhere, that: "I claim you' you are Mine. *Your* Majestic One, your own King." Depression is one of Satan's own tools, and I have found at times that the only effective thing was to command Satan in the name of the Lord Jesus to leave me alone and in so doing have achieved real peace.

In this day and age? This is the twentieth century!

Exactly. And whoever suggested that the devil had gone offstage at the close of the first? America is rife with Satan-worship, witchcraft and demonology. Heaven and angels are real but so are hell and its black hordes, and they can fight us and do, using whatever tools come to hand.

Jealousy is so ugly an emotion that the Bible says it's "cruel as death," and in secular terminology it's the green-eyed monster. Monster it is, but have you ever considered it as idolatry? Strong word, that. The Lord has been dealing with me on this slimy, nasty trait by showing me that if I'm jealous of someone because he or she is receiving some attention, some good time, or some gesture of affection I want (which the giver has every right to give to someone else), I'm coveting, desiring something *not mine*. And that, Paul says, is idolatry. (There is a legitimate place for jealousy: a wife might be understandably upset if hubby began kissing the cute blonde next door. Those kisses are her own prerogative. But that's a different story.) This all ties in with allowing our friends and loved ones to be themselves. We women do have such an inveterate, ingrained habit of trying to remake those we love in our image! Why *shouldn't* my best friend, or sister, or boyfriend for that matter, spend some time with other people, like to be with them *without me*, even show them a brand of attention I don't receive? Can any of us be all things to even one person *all* the time? Would we want to be? Why should I feel I am so fascinating, many-faceted and magnetic that anyone wants to spend every waking hour with me! If the boyfriend wants to spend some time with a buddy, (or even with another girl if you're not pinned or engaged), *you* find someone else pro tem; not in the spirit of tit-for-tat-I'll-get-even-with-you-brother, but realizing he must just now need something the other person gives, and loving him enough to give him freedom to be himself. Let's let our friends "fill our needs but not our emptiness." Hard? You bet it's hard. It's impossible unless we let Christ and His love fill our emptiness.

Remember, if we're feeling left out He says, "He that touches you touches the apple of My eye," and that's warm and protective and personal. We can ask God to release us from whatever is sick, cloying, self-centered in our relationships, not just from our viewpoint, but *from His*. We can ask that as He looks down on our situation, He will change that in us which needs changing. It's a resetting of priorities; a question not only of His dealing with the negatives in us (pride, jealousy, self-centeredness, lack of love), but adding His positives (love, self-giving, generosity). If your negative reaction in a relationship is making shreds and shards of your personality and you're getting your priorities all mixed up, maybe a reanalysis is overdue. *Who* has the right to your top priority, your deepest love, your adoration?

What about my hostilities? Can He free me of these? Can He help me recognize these?

You do understand that I am not playing at being amateur psychiatrist? Deeply imbedded hostilities, along with other root problems, may need professional help, but many of us have things that the Holy Spirit can and will point out and heal if we will just turn to Him. Do we realize the implacable hostility of our natural self and mind to God? Do we think this is something we got rid of at salvation or that it left us forever at a point of surrender? I was shaken when I realized that when Paul writes about the natural mind being enmity against God, it is *my* mind — now — he meant. To some extent it will ride us to the grave.

Hostility to another human being can come from some threat to our identity: by criticism, rejection, or ridicule you may reflect back to me a self-image that makes me feel I am an unworthy person; I react with hostility. If we immerse ourselves in God's love for us, in *His* image of us as totally "accepted in the Beloved," we do not need to react with hostility, anger, or anxiety. He says: "Thou art *all* fair, My Beloved." "The Lord thy God rejoices over *Thee*." So you're not treated with the kindness you deserve? He loves and understands you completely.

For your own preservation keep in mind that hate, bitterness, and malice are prime destroyers of — you. The Bible is practical; sometimes the rhythm and familiarity of some verses make us miss the intense revelance. When we read: "Let there be no more resentment, no more anger or temper, no more violent self-assertiveness (oh?), no more slander and no more malicious remarks," we're apt to feel that Paul is checking over our little hang-ups and urging us to be plaster saints; that God is saying, "No, no; naughty, naughty! You must not lose your temper; that's not nice." Actually, this was two thousand years ahead of the contemporary psychiatrist who tells you that these emotions are destructive and can cause illness in your body and poison in your mind. When will we learn that God's not out of date?

But what do I do about those people I just can't love? You know, the ones who make me all huffy the moment they come on the scene?

Hmm, yes, I'm afraid I do know. It's not easy, and the only solution I have found that works is to be quite honest before the Lord: tell Him we know we are wrong; that we know we should love them but can't even like them, and please will He change us? The verse He gave me in one past battle was startling: "A new heart (that bad?) will I give you, and a new spirit will I put within you: and I will take away the stony heart out of your flesh and give you a heart of flesh."

P.S. When *He* does the changing, it works. Today this particular individual whom I found so difficult is one of my dear friends.

This is all very well, but what about me? I've not only never been loved: I've never even had one boyfriend.

For you my heart aches, and I could wish there were some easy answer, some course one could take, some magic elixir. I pray there may be something somewhere in this limited little book that might open a window which might give you the glimmering of an idea or two.

No point in sugar-coating or glossing it over; it's hard. However, if you slide into the bog of self-pity, you're done, girl. Nothing is more poisonous to the human soul and spirit than this destructive malady which is almost as widespread as the common cold. Nothing is less calculated to bring you the very thing you need: love, not pity.

I'm not about to tell you that there's any easy solution or that going without a solution is easy either. I could urge you to seek competent counsel, but unless that counsel is not only concerned but loving it's not apt to be of any lasting value. Ask the Lord to show you where to turn; He can lead you to some wise and loving person, perhaps someone professionally trained who, with His Spirit's guidance, can uncover the root of the matter: *why* have you never been able to relate to members of the opposite sex? This is a highly individual thing and may well be something deep in the roots of your past, in areas so well-hidden, so expertly defended by you that no one but a Christian professional can uncover it. Please notice I say Christian; only one indwelt by the Third Person of the Trinity is *fully* competent and *thoroughly* equipped. So find a *good* Christian man or woman in the field of counseling; your pastor may be able to help you himself or direct you to one who can. And please don't feel there's any stigma attached to this; you don't hesitate to go to a doctor for physical ailments. With all today's skills, it's folly not to avail yourself of the services of gifted people.

Not everyone needs this. Beware of making it a cult, the "in" thing to do ("And I said to my psychiatrist . . ."). Do all the things you know *you* can do: reevaluate your own attitudes, appearance, interests. Are you an interesting and, above all, a loving person to be with? Giving love requires that we receive love on some level, doesn't it? Maybe our big mistake is trying to drive the car downhill and backwards. *Take in* the glorious fact of Christ's love for you; saturate yourself in the knowledge that you — *you* are His very own. It's only as our hearts are satisfied and filled from the Fountain of all love that we can reach the stage of outgoing, self-giving love to others. As you read over the familiar First Corinthians 13, don't try to whip up in yourself this kind of love; you haven't got it; no one has. Those qualities are only found in Christ's love, and only as we allow His great freshets to course through us will we know anything about this kind of loving. When we do, when He loves others through us, we will know something of being loved in return on a human level. Isn't it a beautiful thing God does for us? *He* gives us the love in the first place; then as it runs through us to others, *we* get human love back in return; then the praise goes back up to Him and the circuit is complete!

But I have this thing about being alone and — I get so scared!

Yes, but He understands this as He understands everything else about you. And He does not get mad at you for feeling like this; He is not condemming you. All the negatives in your personality were dealt with judicially at Calvary; He has no anger left for your failures.

Not for flat-out rebellion?

Perhaps. But even there, in my own life, the thing that eventually has broken me down seemed always to be the great love He showed me. David found this: "Thy gentleness has made me great." It's when we stay in His Presence until His Majesty and wonder strike deep, until we realize that it was *that* God who became Man, who really suffered on a real day in real heat in Jerusalem when there were flies, dust, hatred-you-could-reach-out-and-touch, red wet blood, and knifing pain, when we know this was going on because He cared for us: this is when our stiff rusted wills give way, the barricaded hearts break, and we bow once more.

This fear thing and, closely allied with that, loneliness. I have no idea how many times the words "Fear not" come up in the Bible, but it certainly is often enough for it to finally begin to get through to us that we're just not to be afraid; He *will* be with us; He *will* help and in practical ways. "Fear not; you never shall be put to shame; be not confused, for you shall not be confounded . . . *nothing* need you fear."

But what about my loneliness? Do you know anything about that? Does He?

You mean when you walk out under the sky and there is no one in all the world who really *belongs* to you, that you belong to; when the knife of betrayal stabs the wounds of solitariness; when you walk in the door at night and the silence around you is like a thick, gray shroud and there is no voice, no voice at all? He understands; He is *there*. Not just in some vague theoretical sense, but there; a Person to talk to, to feel, to sense. We can say, "Lord, make me feel this. Speak to my heart that hurts so much just now." A good friend of mine likes to say: "Lord, tell me something nice." When our hearts are empty and no one is around to care, is it a question of psyching ourselves out, of talking ourselves into the idea that Someone is there, that Someone cares? That wouldn't really be much help, would it? No, it's Reality. If God is true, if the Bible means what it says, then Christ is a real, warm, vital Person who understands, who can communicate with us today, whose love is no less real because we cannot at this moment look into His eyes and see it there.

If He has called you to aloneness — and sometimes He does — it's bound to involve loneliness (and they are not the same thing). You may go through many aching hours, oceans of tears in your agonizing struggle toward the completeness found only in Him at last, but is He not, in a sense, paying you a great compliment by asking you to share a state He knew all too well? If He calls you to this, He plans to fill in the gaps with Himself. He says to the few of you who can bear it: If you let Me, I will make up to you *all* losses. Why was He so quick to promise His loved ones (you!) companionship, the comfort of His presence, if it were not that He knew the ache of loneliness, the lack of understanding? "As the sufferings of Christ abound in us so also the consolations abound in Christ." To whatever tiny extent we may experience the things that hurt Him, loneliness, humiliation, rejection, His consolations abound in *that* area!

Here's a thought that will probably mean something to only a few of you: In heaven where there will be no marriage, each of us, man or woman, is going to be an entity in perfect communion with the Lord who created us. Are you willing to be pushed into the Advanced Course now? You have two possible reactions, it seems to me:

1. Well! If heaven isn't going to have marriage, let me get onto the bandwagon here and now!
   or
2. Lord, if You have judged me worthy of this form of fellowship with Your sufferings (and who would know better that it *is* suffering), then I accept the compliment for as long as You choose.

And keep in mind: Joy is the Christian heritage. Complaining is a sin against the living Lord, but joy is His special gift. He says He will give you *His* peace and joy.

(Joy, not happiness. Happiness is a by-product of living, a temporary state that bubbles up inside us at one time but is wiped out the next. Joy is the deep, quiet undercurrent that has its source in the eternal river of God Himself and His peace. That kind of joy can even underlie grief.) Surrounded by people who did not and would not understand, people who made fun, who followed for hedonistic reasons, who were cowardly and disloyal, the homeless Lord of heaven said, "My *joy* I give you, that your joy may be full!"

The very fact that He remained single by choice makes Him able to understand your problem so that you can never say to Him, "You don't know how it is to feel lonely and unwanted." (When many turned and left Him one day, do you remember the wistful remark He made to His disciples: "Will you also go away?" A question to break the heart.)

Joy is deep and gaiety is infectious. We Christians should draw like a magnet because of all the joy we have. I chuckle over Nehemiah 8:12: They made *great mirth* — Why? — because they "*understood* the words (of the Lord) that were declared unto them."

13

Whose Telephone's Ringing Off The Hook?

Can you honestly believe in your heart that God means what He says, that He will *not* withhold good in your life, that He wants to give you a fulfilled and rich life outside marriage?

Maybe you're standing at a sort of crossroad: trained for one thing, doing another, and wondering if you shouldn't be doing some unnamed and unresolved third. You ask yourself whether you are patiently to accept a role which leaves you less-than-fulfilled or seek something which would give you a sense of worth. You've gone over your attitudes and perhaps found that in many ways you've improved greatly, but there is still an unsatisfied longing to *be* somebody, to fill a niche of your own which no one else can fill. There *is* that niche; God doesn't make us

as individuals and then throw us down like so many marbles, each to roll off and find her own place by chance.
What are the problems here?

1. To know your own value.
2. To find a place for that value.
3. To know what God wants you to do about it.

1. The value we've discussed in Chapters One and Two. If you are that important to God, can you not accept yourself as having real worth? If the Lord of all the earth, the Almighty, thought you of such value that He came the long, lonely road from Glory to Golgotha, who are you to disagree with Him?

2. To find a place. Don't set your sights within *your* limited vision; let Him guide your thoughts, and reach for the stars — His stars.

Who, me? I'm just a two-bit typist from Montana. C's all through high school — well, failed a couple of courses, actually. What kind of vision should I have?

"Where there is no vision . . . ." You can go on treadmilling in a squirrelly existence, or you can catch fire by the force of ideas He gives you and then set out to *do* something about it, which is

Point 3. Practical suggestions? Right. Out with the pencil and paper. In one column line up the things you'd *love* to do. Never mind if it seems crazy; we're talking about visions. Opposite each one of these ideas jot down any qualifications you have: training, latent abilities, experience. In another column note the difficulties: finances, educational lacks, probabilities, and so on. Now your last column is important: Is this a field that you can pursue with God's blessing? You certainly don't have to be a missionary; God can use many different kinds of workmen, but there are some things that might seem appealing at first glance that wouldn't be just the thing for the King's daughter. For instance (to go to extremes): the large monetary returns in owning your own liquor store or the glamour of being a cabaret dancer might be dreams you could put an X through in that last column. What's your criterion here, anyway? "Do all things for the glory of God." All things? That's what it says; He even includes eating and drinking.

Now. Everything written down? Any lingering dreams left? Bring them along and let's consider.

Which is your top priority, the one thing you'd love to do or be above everything else? Check out your possibilities. (You'd like to be a lady Leonardo but you can't draw a straight line? This is where practicality enters!) Suppose you'd love to be a teacher, but the education's way beyond your budget; you can't see where you'd get time to study, and what's the use? My suggestion is that you talk to the Lord about it and ask Him if this has anything to do with what He wants for your life. If you begin to feel, in the quiet of your heart, that well, maybe — start things moving. Making a start is important. Ever try steering a parked car? He'll guide you. Start inquiries; not just idle questions posed to people who may know a little, but definite inquiries of people in the field who will have something authoritative to tell you. Write to various universities; find out about scholarships; check your state university; look into night courses and student loans. Private schools sometimes put more emphasis on outstanding people for their faculty than on academic background; check this out. Keep praying. If this is where God wants you, the obstacles will disappear — maybe not as fast as you'd like them to, but they'll go.

Try some vocational guidance tests. Never mind if you've been out of school for ten years; find out where you can take them. This could turn up aptitudes that you didn't know you had or point out to you why you've been

127

unhappy in your present job.

Go to your local library; talk with the librarian about what information is available on vocations, what fields are overcrowded, where the shortages are. If, for instance, you are a violinist and are finding your field discouragingly overcrowded, how about switching to viola? There's a wider scope in most places, and viola's a lovely instrument! Or if you're not making a good living designing upholstery fabrics, what about children's designs? These examples are in related fields, but God may switch you into a totally unrelated one. Include Him in all this; it's folly not to. He can save you enormous amounts of time, wasted energy, and heartache.

Don't sit and wait for lightning to strike. Even if the direction seems totally impractical but oh-so-interesting, move toward it as if it were a possibility and let God stop you if it's not right. Finances loom large on our horizon, but they are very little problem to Him once we line up our priorities. I think we Christians often miss out on a vitally exciting area of living because we insist on being pragmatic in this area. We may trust God in every other area of our lives, but in this *we* know best; we're sure there's only one way to approach this problem, and we lose two things in one checkbook: the thrill of finding out what God can do and the pleasure He would have in surprising us!

One of the most beautiful and touching things that happened while I was waiting in the States to come to L'Abri involved finances. My passage money was to come from the sale of my grand piano and my car. The piano, the best I had ever owned, would not sell; the car was totalled in a wreck and the insurance settlement, as is the way with insurance settlements these days, tarried exceeding long! During this time I was doing a lot of reevaluating, thinking, and praying. Had I got my wires crossed? Still sure that L'Abri was where God was directing me, I became convinced that the money from *both* these items (when it came) was to go for something else! I knew this was of the Lord, but I did tend to ask, "Lord, are you sure? You know this is all I have for passage money and . . . ." He was, as He is in His magnificently gentle way, relentless. Meanwhile, unknown to me, someone had made a quiet bargain with the Lord; the profit from the sale of a car would go to me *if* God gave her a certain clear sign. This involved giving up a stereo set much desired by her teen-age children. She talked it over with them, and the fourteen-year-old boy, seeing his dream-stereo vanishing into the sunset, still said, "Let's do it; you can't outgive the Lord." The sign came; I was overwhelmed with the gift of the passage money and its encouragement and — are you ready for this? — two weeks later the kids received a beautiful stereo from someone in a distant state!

Fairy story! Visionary! Impractical! What is this, first century christianity?

The same God who did the first century miracles, to be sure; the same God who walked on the waters in a consummate disregard of His own natural laws; the God-who-is-Enough. *Your* God in *your* century. I'm no special person; I'm someone with more faults than average, with wide streaks of weakness that are made worse by the fact that people don't always see them, and so I make things aggravated by being proud of *that!* No, lady, He *is* the same yesterday, now, and always.

If you're moaning and groaning because you're stymied at every turn by finances (and who is not at one time or another?), ask God to show you ways in which He can use this to teach you valuable lessons: lessons of dependence, of stewardship, of management. He's a practical God, and that key principle in Malachi 3 of bringing Him His due portion *first* brings remarkable blessing. You can be glad if you're not affluent because you have an opportunity to throw this problem of finances on the Lord and watch Him make a miracle for you. (Sometimes the miracle will be showing you how to cut corners!) This is a sphere in which God delights to demonstrate who He is, and people who never know financial worries miss out on some exciting demonstrations of His concern.

Well, I'm satisfied with my career. It's all the free time that's getting me down. With all this energy and all that love dammed up inside, what's a girl to do?

Obviously some outlet is imperative, and there are only so many trips abroad one can afford, so many chances to entertain or be entertained. Even the most popular girl may find herself with blank evenings and wonder what to do with them.

Creativity is vital to the thinking human being, some form of creativity. It can range from painting a masterpiece to baking an apple pie, but we have a built-in need to fashion something we can look at and say, "That's mine; *I* did it!"

Speaking of apple pies: if you like cooking, you probably won't need any urging to entertain, but how about having a few girls in who'd love to learn how to cook? Many girls coming here to Switzerland know nothing about cooking but enjoy learning in the everyday routine. (Our classic about a girl who became a fine cook goes back to her initial days when she didn't know how to boil water. She was sent out to the garden for carrots and came back saying, "There aren't any; I looked everywhere and there was nothing orange in sight.")

Why not create interesting things with a group that likes to sew or work with felt (with felt you can do *anything*). Not artsy-craftsy posy-holders or frilly nothings but contemporary linens, stunning wall hangings, brilliant holiday tablecloths or things of wood and metal. You'll have fun making them together, sharing ideas, and then selling them privately or through some store. Have a showing: serve coffee, sell pastries. Snoop around some of the gift stores in town, the snootier the better; you'll find ideas by the dozen for things you can make.

One obvious place to start some creative activity is in your own church group. There are people there of your own age who love the Lord too. No good group? You have two choices: get one going or, if that fails, look for another church. I do not mean that one's church *affiliation* is primarily social. However, if you are finding absolutely no fellowship in your church, you might prayerfully consider finding another church which is sound not only in its doctrine, but also in its community. To stay in a sterile church until your own enthusiasm dries up or until, in a confusion of issues, you begin to question the validity of the Christian faith is madness.

In or out of the church setting, what about cell groups of people your age who have common interests: art, music, literature, Bible study, language study, discussions of all sorts? One bright gal I heard about started groups in a local restaurant. They meet for coffee or a meal and deliberately avoid the church connotation. For many people today the very idea of "church" turns them off, so if your group is comprised of these keep it outside the church and wait until they *ask* to go to a service or study group. You could be careful not to conflict with service times; a small group can meet in your room, a larger one at the local coffee shop.

Certainly one of the great lacks in the life of the single girl is family life. In spite of the current swing away from this vital block in any nation's building, it remains God's foundation for society. Cell groups can bring a sense of belonging, and from these can grow a Christian community that will deepen this sense. They can make a fulfilling substitute and bring fewer, or at least different, responsibilities. "He sets the solitary in families," does not necessarily mean He is going to give you a husband and children of your own, but if you look to Him for an implementation of this promise, He will set you in some sort of family somewhere that is exactly suited to your needs.

What about a Christian art community? It can consist of three people. Near L'Abri one enterprising couple rented an old house where he makes beautiful furniture and a friend who's moved in with them paints pictures. The wife is the spark who gives enthusiasm, criticism, encouragement, and great food. When they complete a number of things, they invite people in and the word spreads.

You're a musician? Share your music. Don't feel it *must* be in the usual "sacred" framework; all beautiful things fit in with the truth of things as they are, as God made them. Start a folk-singing group, try your hand at original songs, songs perhaps with a Christian emphasis (but please, not corny, not nineteenth century; make it your generation's voice). Get a discussion going on the philosophy behind contemporary music (pop, rock, or classical). What is the musician saying? What's the difference between the romantic (in the worst sense of the word) jingly hymns or ballads of the last century and the brutal indictments of a Bob Dylan? Or try a hymn-writing contest; there are almost no really fine tunes being written. What has happened that Christian art and music are now synonymous with mediocrity? They are, you know, and you could be the revolutionary who turns the tide.

No talents? Not artistic? For one thing, let's drop this idea that the arts constitute all that is meant by the word talent. I've been a professional musician most of my adult life, but I feel we're far too narrow if we consider only the artistic disciplines as talents. A person who inspires artists is talented, a person who creates a lovely home atmosphere is talented, so is a person who cooks a fine meal, and a person who listens to others has a special — and rare — talent.

Do try to escape the TV-itis that afflicts so many, or the I-just-don't-have-time-for-anything routine. *Make* time as if your life were at stake, for in one sense, it is.

I haven't mentioned the many Christian groups you could align yourself with; many of you know about these. Perhaps all you can do is offer your home: Offer it!

Black or white, you may feel strongly about the race situation: as a Christian girl what can you do? As a start, be sure your own life demonstrates the love and equality you say you feel for the other race. In America today all kinds of tacks are being taken, but here, as in every other field, the Christian approach *should* be the best. (Regrettably, this is often far from true.) Can you show love not only to the whites and blacks who are the underdogs in your neighborhood, office, or school, but also to the militants? We can take a stand, must take a stand against wrong where we see it and where it conflicts with God's standards, but that doesn't mean lack of love to *people,* ever, no matter how wrong we may feel their actions to be. And for those of you shouting: *"Tolerance! We want tolerance!" "Where's the Christian ideal of tolerance?"* (for blacks, whites, Women's Lib, student rioters), be sure *you are* tolerant of the intolerants. There's the command to pray for *all* men, including the WASPS you find so smug and infuriating. Tolerance, real tolerance, takes the grace of God.

Do we really believe God can and will demonstrate His power today in our puny lives? Since the first century there may not have been a time when there was a greater opportunity for us to prove Him. Many of us believe that in the foreseeable future Christians will be facing the greatest challenge of their lives. "Who is on the Lord's side?" is not going to be some pleasant little chorus to sing on Sunday nights, but a resounding rallying cry of the Mighty Champion who really is going to dominate the whole earth — your part of it: Phoenix, Cedar Falls, and Hackensack, among others. Before this happens we will again be the unpopular minority out of the mainstream, given an opportunity unprecedented in modern times to stand clearly for the living God, though it be death. All the years I was growing up, and for many years thereafter, Christian martyrdom was something one read about in the New Testament or in books about Christian pioneers in far away lands like Tasmania. The assassination of the five men in Ecuador rocked us. In the twentieth Century? But how many have died for the faith since? Make no mistake, there will be other Christian martyrs. This may seem remote to you in your comfortable existence in the 1970s in America, but not if you really understand the totality of the decay around you, the disintegration of any straight-line values. This is happening with scary rapidity.

The other evening I stood watching a spectacular sunset which in seconds was obliterated by clouds which boiled up from the valley below. Today the mists of relativistic thinking, poisoned with rebellion against the God-of-absolutes, threaten to do the same thing with the light of the Christian revelation and are fast obscuring the outlines of our familiar guideposts. We need to be asking God what He wants us to do to be preparing ourselves and those we love for the days that lie ahead, to be praying for strength to remain strong in the faith. During the sixties we built bomb shelters in case of attacks that never came; as Christian women we may well be really concerning ourselves with spiritual bomb shelters for the rough times that *will* come, that are Scripturally predicted. What does this involve? As single women you are much freer to engage in this sort of activity and you have more scope.

1. Preparedness on a personal level: a strengthening of spiritual muscles by exercise and much nourishment from God's revelation and a much deeper commitment to Jesus Christ. Paul's words have a distinctly contemporary flavor: "Every contact with the world must be as light as possible, for the present scheme of things is rapidly passing away." As we see Christian basics going down the drain (and please do *look*; be aware of what *is* happening), we can understand something of what he meant.

2. Communication with others. Helping to prepare others: a sister, a girlfriend, a co-worker — whoever God sends you. This could be an in-depth Bible study, memorizing Scripture (have you thought what it would be like to have no Bible available?), praying together, really expecting God to use your lives as a living showcase for His power. Your life, in its individual connotation as well as its communal one, is an object lesson for angelic beings! God is using us to demonstrate His power to them. "The purpose is that all the angelic powers should now see the complex wisdom of God's plan being worked out through the Church!" Your very singleness can be a glowing witness of the power of Christ to overcome even this obstacle; He can use *you* as a successful experiment to the angels. They must lean over the balustrade of heaven with amazement as they see what He can do with fragile human lives!

3. A vital community life perhaps growing from the cell groups which under God could develop into a a shining beacon on a hill proclaiming: God IS!

4. Finally, God's ministry for each of us is surely love. The love between a man and woman is only one kind of love. The fact that there are so many bitter, dried-up spinsters in the world is not due primarily to the fact of their singleness, but because having been denied married love, they have sulkily shut them-

selves up from all the other beautiful varieties of God's greatest gift.

Remember Isaiah 54:1? "More are the children of the desolate than the children of the married wife." I know people in middle life who have never married who have spiritual children scattered all over the globe and whose family grows continually; their correspondence is enormous. They lead happy and fulfilled lives because they have learned to love.

Friendship has been called the most unselfish form of love there is. There are children, old people, young drifters, your contemporaries, harried housewives lonely in the midst of humdrumness. God is looking for channels. Anyone of any age of any race of any education can be a pipeline for the flow of His love. "You shall be like a watered garden, an oasis with a steadfast spring." Allow Him to clear out whatever is clogging your spring and permit His great surge of love to pour through you to a world that is parched and dying for lack of it.

14

Are You So Glad You're Not Young Anymore?

Is God to blame that you're still single after all these years? Is it His fault? Since He made you as you are with your drives, hopes, longings, and at least some of your dreams, it doesn't make sense that He would turn around and willfully frustrate you. Intellectually you know about trusting God; how about emotionally?

Going back to square one: you can't trust your life to someone you haven't spent much time cultivating or knowing in the heart-sense of that word. It is the "people that do *know* their God" who will be strong and do exploits.

Maybe you're shouting so loud God can't get through. If you're spending a lot of time fighting God on this issue of singleness, you're going to make hash of both possibilities for your life: you'll be

137

neither good wife-material nor an interesting singleton.

If you've been rejected, thrown over, turned down, it may be small comfort to you that you have lots of company, but what's your attitude *now*? Today? Are you Miss Havisham in *Great Expectations*, wrapping yourself in the frayed draperies of the past, sitting in the mental dark, playing your one-string tune over and over?

What, after all, are your choices?

1. You sulk and fume inwardly and become frustrated, bitter, unattractive.
   (You may do this; God won't interfere with your freedom of choice.)
2. You grab yourself a man — any man — so you will have "made it."
   (You may do this, too; *some* man is probably available, and the chances are God won't stop you, but prepare yourself for some rough times.)
3. You positively commit this area to God and trust Him to lead you into the vital, dynamic life He wants you to have.

Have you considered the beauty there can be in an understanding companionship with a man? You'll have to be careful here or you may make a man feel you're out to get him (and let's be honest, too often we are). Create an atmosphere of trust and friendship with the men God does bring along; enjoy them and thank God for the richness they add to your life. Don't miss today's blessings for some mirage of possible connubial bliss!

Should you reach the place where you find yourself considering marriage with one of these friends, do be realistic. Don't refuse, out-of-hand, to marry some friend you know as "solid and dependable" but hardly exciting. How much excitement do you want? Would you really enjoy a dashing, importunate Romeo who kept your life in an uproar, who wanted your body six nights out of seven? Can you fit yourself into this picture?

Understanding, sharing, deep quiet love shot through with some fire — isn't this what you want? Marriage is certainly best for this, but if God sends you a friend who will bring you even some of these things, don't boorishly push His hand away with, "Where's that Lochinvar I've been asking You for all these years?" Maybe you just haven't recognized him. Lochinvar, that is. Someone has said that the beginning of all rebellion against God is a failure to say "Thank You." It's so like us to concentrate on what we *don't* have or what we'd like to have and ignore completely so much that He has given us.

May I suggest: don't try to compete with the youngsters on their territory; you can't. Who's kidding who? Their skin is smooth and lovely; yours may have had it. Their figures are dreamy; yours may be a nightmare. *(That* you can improve, however.) You can't match 'em so don't even try to join 'em. However neither should you underrate the decided edge God and time have given you in other areas: understanding, sensitivity, unselfishness (we hope), experience, maturity, charm. Young people have enormous zest, sex-appeal and a quality all their own, but remember your own uniqueness which *they* can't counterfeit. A girl of twenty may give a man of forty-five much excitement, but she may not bring him deep understanding; and understanding is something one hungers for as much in maturity as one did in youth. (Note: European men seem to understand better than most Americans that the qualities of charm and ·fascination, like some beverages, tend to improve with aging! At least, one likes to think they do!)

Speaking of sex-appeal: *watch it!* If you grow desperate, you could be trapped by this even more than the kids. A man may exert a tremendous attraction physically and be pretty poor husband material. Friendship, mutual liking, all-round compatability, and, above all, spiritual depth — these things are the bedrock in a good marriage at any age, the things we live with day after day. Romance and physical magnetism add the zest that makes the day-by-day-ness bearable, but a lifetime with nothing to support the zest could be a *long* time!

Do you want a man of God and God's man for you so much that you are willing to trust God even if the man He brings into your orbit is not as exciting as you had hoped? Can God, in other words, teach you to love, change your heart?

What a goofy idea! You can't manipulate your heart! You can hold yourself to a certain course of action, I suppose, but you can't rule your heart!

I didn't say you; I said God.

Can He take out of your heart an unsuitable love, one not His best choice for you, and give you a tremendous feeling for someone you never thought you could love *that* way? Well, is He the Sovereign of your life? If so, is there any area He isn't capable of changing if you trust Him enough to hand Him the key?

A dear friend of mine, a widow who had deeply loved her husband, was being ardently pursued by a fine Christian man. She simply was not interested. Admiration she had — friendly, warm feelings — but he did not excite her. Time passed — a number of years, in fact; she began to consider marrying for her children's sake, but still, no great passion. More time went by (she was out of her thirties, by the way); they began to pray together. Then she wrote me, "We are sure now what *we* want, but we are waiting to be sure we have God's green light to go ahead." The end of that story is that about a year later she was saying, "I never thought I could love anyone so much!" and yes, of course she married him. Can you trust God that much? If marriage is God's choice for you, you won't have to settle for some "marriage of convenience";

it will *not* be something second-rate.

You singles have another area in which you can excel if you want to, and that is in a personal walk with the Lord. You have time to develop an in-depth relationship.

Who has time? I work; commute; do all my own housework . . . .

Yes, I do know; I've been there. And yet, be honest. What about all those evenings when the phone doesn't ring and you have no place to go and no one to talk to? They can be tough nights, I agree; I've had many more of these nights than "togetherness" nights. But you can go grumbling to your tent, you can live vicariously through TV, or you can be like a sharp girl of twenty-four who recently wrote me: "I'm home from work really looking forward to a good quiet evening with the Lord." Have you learned this reality?

Remember me? I'm a human being, very frail, very physical. I'm not just spirit.

Right you are. Though each of us is different, the basic needs are the same. The interest in sex does not disappear, but our deeper hunger is for tenderness and strength, for being held and treasured because we are "us." Someone has done a study on us women and discovered that this need to be held is so deep-rooted in our nature that it is often the reason girls and women give themselves to a man physically. What a lot of heartache could be saved if we — and men — understood this better!

But what do we *do* when the ache to be touched, when the longing to feel strong arms around us, grows all but too sharp to bear? A young girl here who had had more way-out experience in suffering than most people know in a lifetime spoke to this problem. She had been ill and she said, "I just wanted someone's arms around me and there wasn't anyone. So I said, 'Lord, You'll just have to put Your arms around me,' and you know what? He did."

Impractical? Imaginative? Escapism? Not if our God is *real.*

On the human level, I wonder if we can't find some healing in transferring this longing, in *giving* what we would like to be receiving. We don't need to look far to find some child, some young person whose loneliness and fear needs the comfort of our touch, of being held a moment in our arms.

How honest have we been with God in this matter of our solitariness? Our responsibility as individuals who choose is greater than we like to admit. Perhaps we've faced crises, turning points of great significance which we failed to recognize simply because we were not listening or were not where He could guide us with His eye. I know this has been true in my own life. William Golding in *Free Fall* speaks of the "decision freely made that cost me my freedom." As you look back over the years, are there some wrong turnings when God might have liked to tell you something, when He spoke in His still, small voice and you didn't hear? He doesn't shout; He refuses to invade your privacy, to trample your personality. How many times may your deafness have changed the course of your personal history? We fail here, and some years later come awake with a jolt to find we're far from home and our Father's house, and we wonder why. "Like a crooked arrow they missed the target of God's will . . . the girls had never a wedding song."

Perhaps you've been working away on a mission field, working so hard you've never slowed down for God's *current* directive, or you've sacrificed everything and are staying at home with an elderly father. As painful as it may be, try to go back to the place where you may have made choices you *thought* were God's will; ask Him to show you whether it was this in fact or whether you were pressured by other people:

> "Isn't it *magnificent* to see Julia going to Africa! That will make the twelfth from our church!"
> "Mary, dear! You can't marry *that* man! He's just not good enough for you, darling!"
> or
> "Ellen's place is with her poor, dear father; that's as plain as the nose on your face."

When you decided you must sacrifice your life for daddy (and be applauded as a devoted daughter?), *might* it not have been better for dad (as well as for you) to be in a Christian home with his cronies playing chess or shuffleboard instead of being bored with you and your growing bitterness?

As I dodge brickbats from irate daughters and lady missionaries, let me say I *know* this is not always true; I *know* there are many of you who are in the place God placed you. But if you are one of these, why so upset? God's will brings peace, and when we're where *He* puts us, we have serenity. (No, not every moment.) If we lack these qualities, one of two things can be wrong; the place or our attitude.

This dame's really mixed up! What good is it going to do even if I do search the past and let God show me if — and where — I made a wrong turning? Even God's not going to turn back the clock.

No, He's not, but He may want to show you, very gently, what attitude of mind and heart caused the wrong turning and show you that this attitude has changed very little. He wants to come into the labyrinth of your personality and challenge the locked-in-ness of your heart. The circumstances *may* have to stay as they are, but remember you are dealing with the God who does wonders. He can change *you* and will if you let Him. None of us have to be what we are now, what we were ten years ago, last year, or even last week.

The problem that plagues most of us is this getting still before our God and letting Him search us and show us what's out of kilter. This is usually an uncomfortable and upsetting process. We are afraid to be shown and carefully squirrel things in corners lest He point out to us that *this* thing has to go. "My mind is made up; don't confuse me with facts."

Do you suppose in the beauty of the life to come He may show us what He wanted to give us, and we'll look down and see in our hands the thing, dried up and dusty, that we would not release to Him, the thing that seemed so precious and important. We'll wonder with amazement how we could have been so blind. Or perhaps in our "very own room" there we'll find some lovely thing that we had longed to have, some talent even, or a friendship; and He'll tenderly point out to us that He would have given it to us long before, but we were so niggardly with our trust that He couldn't and it had to wait. Pure fantasy — I suppose.

It's a secret of letting go, isn't it, and of being able to say David's shatteringly difficult prayer: Search me, O God, and know my heart; try me and know my thoughts, and *see* if I am taking a wrong course and — lead me.

The man of God may have a different answer to that one, but as women our hearts must be involved in this as well as our wills. It's no good saying, "I must yield, I must, I *must!!*" There's a great struggle that ensues, a cacophony starts up inside us, and the battle is on! Is your will stamping its feet, throwing itself on the floor in a fit, and screaming? You may have thought some area quite committed and be shocked by the violence of your reactions when He challenges your right to keep it. The old Satanic lie comes to us: "*Has* God said? He doesn't want to make you happy; He doesn't really understand." But it is when Christ comes to us, when He wordlessly stretches out His scarred hands, that we find ourselves crying out, "How can I deny You anything?" Reasonings, trying to beat your will into submission, to make yourself obedient — no good; but before this Majestic Person the heart and will both bow.

I keep asking myself why you are single, you who long not to be. Some of you have become submerged, and instead of becoming freer as you have gone on in life and in the Lord, the real you has become buried under an exterior of efficiency, of brusqueness that covers sensitivity, a defensive wall you've built up to keep yourself from being hurt. Perhaps you've reached a point where you feel, "I can't take any more; I can't risk another hurt," and you've put up a barbed wire barricade. Funny thing about barbed wire; the spikes point in both directions. They will keep off outward attacks (at the same time hurting well-meaning people who had nothing to do with your original pain), but they wound you inwardly. Allow God to be your defense, and He will cover you with His feathers (how different from spikes!) and no one will get hurt.

Or is it that you have given up hope? Have you reached 28-35-50 and said, "What's the use? No one will want me now?" Aren't you forgetting God? Do you really think He is unable to bring into your life one man who is a child of His who is lonely too, who needs what you have to give, and who could meet your human needs as a woman? The indictment of the Israelites of the Pentateuch was that they *limited* the Holy One of Israel. God, in His respect for the personalities He has made and in the gentleness with which He deals with us, allows us — us — to *limit* what He would like to do for us. Please! If you've been limiting the One who loves you so much, who longs to rejoice over you, to do you good — stop! ("O that My people would listen to Me, that they would live My life!")

Some of you panic inwardly at the thought of marriage. Oh yes, part of the time you think you'd like to be married; it's fun to toy with the idea and spin dreams. When the other girls moan about the problems of singleness, you moan too. Companionship and love, maybe children, seem very appealing, and there are those lovely wedding dreams . . . . But because of some bad experience in your past, you shy like a skittish mare when anything approaching a real possibility rides into view. Or is it a nagging sense of guilt over old sins, or some commitment in which you feel you failed that has made you lose self-confidence?

But God . . . .

"But God who is rich in mercy for the great love wherewith He loves us," He can knit up the frayed ends of the past, the frayed ends of you; He can restore the years that the locust has eaten. If He brings someone into your life who just might be His choice for you, ask for the courage to be open on the God-ward side, to stand on your watch and see what He says to you about this new relationship. It can be a fresh new beginning in the power of God; it just might be God's love-gift to you.

I admit I know next to nothing about advertisements that deal with lonely people who want to meet or correspond with others, but if the Christian publications carry this sort of thing, you could give it a try. Who'd know? If you're edgy about having some creep arrive on your doorstep, suitcase in hand, get a P.O. box and have the mail sent there. Pray about this, of course. I've been told that some good marriages have resulted from this sort of thing.

We lock our hearts' doors with our fears, with our prejudices, and when God comes knocking we can't hear. Let's suppose you're working in Peru, or India, or even Afghanistan. Suppose one of the natives, a real man of God who was a gentleman of fine feeling and sensitivity — suppose he began to show interest in you. What would you do?

146

Apply for a transfer? Wrap yourself in frosty remoteness? Laugh it off? Or would you ask God if *He* had any ideas? (Yes, I do realize there are many problems here, but what I'm pleading for is that you ask the God-of-infinite-imagination what He has in mind for this relationship.)

Is your mind "like concrete: all mixed up and firmly set?" What would you do if you met an attractive man but he was twenty-five years older than you? Or even ten years younger? *Certainly* there are problems, but if it should be God's man knocking at your door, you're going to miss out on a wonderful experience. Don't you even want to know what this man is like? *Never mind* the Ladies' Sewing Circle or the Missionary Guild! This is *your* life! You're never going to please everyone — never. You are God's woman; His servant, yes, but also His princess. Ask *Him* what He wants you to do.

15

Meanwhile, Back At The Farm... Or School-room... Or Office...

For one reason or another you expect to stay single, so what can you do about it?

I think there are two aspects to this problem — two horns of the dilemma. One is practical: how to spend your time, day after day; the other is one of attitude: *how* do you face the possibility of being single the rest of your life. Let's take the easier one first, the practical angle.

How about adopting children? You can, you know. If you don't insist on an infant, I understand there is a fair possibility that a single person can adopt children. One friend of mine ran a nursery school and found herself making a permanent home for two youngsters whose parents did not want them. She is now their legal guardian and having some of the joys of a family even though single.

Courage? You bet it takes courage, but there are thousands of lonely kids in the world for whom one parent is a lot better than none.

Do you recall the opening verse of Isaiah 54: "Sing, O barren, thou that didst not bear . . . more are the children of the desolate than the children of the married wife." Has this become true for you? Do you have spiritual children? God is not only willing, but anxious to give to each of us a special family: those we may bring to birth into His family and/or those we care for as they grow up to be princes in His household. Are you singing even though you have been denied one of womanhood's greatest blessings? You can. He wants to grant you many children who will love you deeply and truly and with whom you will maintain a deep and lasting relationship. Your spiritual children can be closer and more loyal than the physical children of others. Bringing spiritual children into His kingdom is not a special function limited to the missionary, the preacher, or the Sunday school teacher. We are each endowed with the same Holy Spirit, and since it is His life and His work and His love, our opportunities are limitless.

Maybe you have hidden talents. My mother developed an exquisite watercolor technique after she was seventy. Another elderly friend published her first book. Someone else, after years of having long-suffering friends make her clothes and let down hems, developed into a good seamstress. You never know till you try.

Perhaps you've enjoyed making Christmas decorations and gifts for years, but have never thought of this as talent or something God could use. The things you make might be sold or shared with lonely people who are thrilled with a small gift, or you might use your home as a craft center and teach people how you do it. Young people in your neighborhood are sometimes bored and have no idea how to fill in time other than spending hours glued to the TV; housewives you know might need a creative outlet, or you might change the whole outlook for some old people. There are classes in almost anything, from folk dancing to weaving, from pottery-making to serious painting and creative writing.

You feel you have no creative ability at all? Few people really fall into this category; we are all children of the Creator: God. Ask the One who created you what His ideas are for you. But again: we must always come in faith; we can't waver and suggest He exhibit a few samples while we decide whether or no we'll condescend to buy. We must ask to be shown that we may get going and *do*. Right?

And please don't give up on your appearance. How do you *know* this isn't the day you'll meet someone interesting? You don't have to supinely accept all you are. It was a cheering day for me when I suddenly realized I didn't have to rejoice over the wrinkles and other signs of age arriving with distressing rapidity. Not for themselves, I don't. Besides — and this is where we Christians have another beautiful bonus — it won't always be this way. It *is* upsetting to see grey coming into the hair, the battle of the bulge being lost, and realizing no one will ever again take us for twenty-five. But the day will come, ladies, when this face will again be as smooth as a rose petal, and there will be no signs in the body I will be living in that sin ever existed! It really is going to happen: you'll really be you, living in a perfect and beautiful body! So, cheers! It's uncomfortable for a time, let's admit, but it's *temporary!*

We need to find a balance between attempting to look a coy twenty-one (which fools nobody and may give rise to some pretty raucous comments) and the staid, unflattering, old-maid-y look that announces: "Abandon hope — I have!"

You who feel the ache of singleness: how about doing something for the many people in the same situation?

Instead of saying, "Why doesn't someone do something for my age group; why is everything so couple-oriented?" *You* be the one to do something. *You* get a lively group organized for singles of both sexes, in or out of your church setting. Pool your imaginations, share your interests and enthusiasms, or constructively discuss your mutual problems. Non-Christians have groups for singles, why not you?

What about the various telephone services that could use your time? There are the ones for potential suicides, for instance, and the sort of thing the Dial-a-Prayer began. Your church may have one going or a group of you could begin one of your own. Publish a phone number somewhere and invite lonely troubled people to call; have one or preferably two people manning the phone four or five hours at a stretch. God will give you some great experiences, and if the problems get too big for you to handle (as they quite possibly will), have as many experts as you can muster on call: a nurse, employment officer, doctor, psychologist, or your own minister.

During World War II I made the acquaintance of the excellent Grey Lady service of the American Red Cross. At the time I was in the middle of a disturbing personal crisis which seemed to fill all my waking thoughts, but as I worked among the tragic casualties at Walter Reed Hospital and was confronted with the courage and humor of the GI's, I found that hours would go by in which I hadn't once thought of my own problems. Hospitals, particularly mental hospitals, have many patients who never have a visitor. One goes expecting to give, but what one gets back is beyond words. Give what you have to God — all you know you have, but also — and this is important — what you think you don't have. Ask Him to use you "as it pleases Him." If you are asked to speak somewhere, don't go into a blue dither and screech: "I can't; I can't possibly; I can't get up in front of four people, let alone . . . ."

Moses and Jeremiah had a similar problem, and the same God who promised to be with their mouths will be with yours. God never assigns us tasks He does not intend to see through with us. Your talk may not sound like the Gettysburg Address, but keep it brief, learn it well, and — pray! In time you may become addicted to speaking!

We can tap our reservoir of unused love; we can let God love through us and pour it out to the people our lives touch. Perhaps never before have kids needed love so desperately. Don't be fooled by "good homes" and both parents being there. There are still really good homes, thank God, but inside other "good" homes there is little love or closeness. You don't understand today's kids? *Learn to!* Give it time and thought and, above all, prayer. Share what God has taught you, yes, but learn how *they* think, what *their* interests are. Get on their wavelength; don't expect them to get on yours. You will get back such a flood of warmth, love, unselfishness, and gratitude that you'll have trouble believing it.

You'd like a home of your very own, wouldn't you? Of course. But not having a husband of your own to share it with is not reason to deny yourself some of the joys this brings. Whatever place you have, even a room, can become a place of charm, warmth, and hospitality. Kids today are in revolt against the affluent society, and they sit on the floor and "make do" by choice. They'll be happy with makeshift furniture, tired old rugs or no rugs, and chipped dishes. Light the candles, put on the coffee, make some cookies, and open your heart. You won't have to talk brilliantly; listen — this is your route to understanding. More than anything else, just love them. There's no therapy for an aching heart like losing oneself in someone else's aching heart.

You have that beautiful stereo set and all those records.

I wouldn't let my own grandmother touch them! Why

that machine cost me a month's wages!

Quite. Don't. But invite people in. You'd be amazed to see a small room here at L'Abri jammed with kids — on the bed, curled up under the sink, sprawled all over the floor; rapt, intent, absolutely quiet, listening to the world's great music because one man shares what he has.

Or get a collection of *their* music and learn with them why they enjoy it.

There must be boys and girls, young men and women you know or whom you could find who need a mother figure. You can make your kitchen a gathering place for the gang to eat, drink coffee, and tell you their troubles. They'll love it, but so will you.

Does that "mother figure" make you squirm? Are we so unwilling to admit honestly where we *are* in life (as opposed to where we would like to be) that we miss out both ways? There are beauties in each stage of life. The Youth Cult in America denies this and cries that only the very young have any fun at all so — Be Young! (Or at least look and act that way!) It takes wisdom from the Lord to know just how far we can go without looking ridiculous and thus shutting ourselves and others away from the riches that go with maturity. These kids need to feel they can trust us, and they are more apt to feel they can if we accept ourselves as we really are.

But I'm a busy career woman. I spend 8 — 10 — 12 hours a day at my job. When I come home at night, all I want to do is get my feet up and watch TV or read.

Well, lady, you can go ahead and do that, but then you mustn't complain about loneliness. Because Solomon was right: To have friends, you must show yourself friendly. People won't come to you unless you draw them with love.

You don't feel comfortable around teen-agers? Not your

cup of tea? What about little children or old people? How about reading aloud to someone? This is a double-barreled blessing: think what exciting literature *you'll* be discovering! What about your own contemporaries or younger people in your field who need your wisdom and experience? Share, lady, share; there's no other way out of loneliness that I know.

Now if the comfort of your solitary life satisfies you, why are you reading this? I would suggest, though, if you have not thrown me across the room, that as a Christian you have both the privilege and the responsibility of sharing. "He that loves his life . . . ." I used to be troubled over lonely and bitter old people: I am still troubled by them, but the Lord showed me a verse one day that explains something, I think: "God brings the lonely home and frees the prisoner for prosperity; *only the rebels have to live forlorn."* Choices again. Today we make the choices in our lives that will determine the kind of old person we will be. May we have compassion on the rebels but, by God's grace, not become one. We're not marionettes, and even though we all can look back to some bad choices, today's can be titanic. We can choose to let God choose, choose to see what He can do with our battered lives. He *can* work miracles today. I know. Notice how often He says, "*I* will do . . . . *I* will heal . . . . *I* will change . . . . *I* will make." There are many places, but as a start try Isaiah 43, 44, 45.

May I remind you gently and with love that the day is coming when we will face our loving Lord; will we then dare to say to Him, "You didn't send me a husband so I withered on the vine"?

Because you are unique, one-of-a-kind and God does not waste His handiwork, there is some particular place He wants to use you. But only He can show you where, when, and how.

Which brings us back full circle to the primary thing:

getting to know your God, spending time in His presence, giving Him the joy of your love, the sound of your voice, your companionship. "Let Me hear *thy* voice, let Me see *thy* countenance, for sweet is thy voice and thy countenance is comely." Yours. No one else's will do, and no service takes the place of this.

And now we come to the tough one: attitude. What is to be my attitude if I've reached the point where I realistically realize I may very well remain single? Whatever the reasons, there are the facts. How can I handle this?

First of all we can admit the difficulty. We don't need to run around saying with a quavery voice and a saccharine smile: "I guess I'm just one of God's unclaimed treasures." We can be honest before God and people and say out loud: "There are things about being single that I don't like at all; there are times when I'd give a lot to be married." But as this attitude is realistic, I think we need also to be realistic about the good aspects of the single life — and it has very good aspects. Freedom is one: freedom to make decisions on all levels, to have things as we enjoy them, to spend our time as we choose, to see whom we like when we like.

There is also mobility. If God opens up a new door (as He is quite likely to do if we give Him half a chance), we often can go at once. If we freely put our time at God's disposal, we may find we have more of it to share than our married sisters.

There is also the area of friendships: a single girl often can have a much wider variety of friends than a wife can.

There is the close bond with a large segment of the population which is also single. At first glance this may seem to be a pretty uninteresting prospect, a sort of misery-loves-company philosophy, but some of the most interesting people I know are single (and I don't mean *just* men!). Often they have developed their minds and skills in a way married people have not had time to do. I don't advocate *just* single friends by any means; this can be sterile. Couples, young and old, families, children, young people — our circle of acquaintances and friends should include all these.

Yes, singleness can be lonely at times, but we need to be realistic about this too and stop feeling sorry for ourselves. Would you exchange your loneliness for the lot of the woman whose husband sleeps around or comes home drunk every night or who never speaks to her except to criticize? You think *you're* lonely!

Do we really mean it when we say, "I want God to use my life," or are we setting limitations? Suppose this book finds you disgruntled over your single lot just now: are you willing to be entirely free before our Father, letting go of all your prejudices and preconceived ideas and telling Him you are ready for Him to give you whatever He wants for the future? It may not be easy. Should He ask, are you willing to relinquish your possessions, to go off to some new environment, some entirely different job? He promises good things, but He never says that it will not be costly.

Can you lose? Remember you are entrusting your future to the One who regards you as something of great value. He says: "The Lord, your God, is in your midst, a warrior who gives victory; he will rejoice over you with gladness; he will *renew* you in his love. He will joy over you with a song of triumph."

There's another challenging verse in Isaiah 54: "Your Maker is your husband, the Lord of hosts is his name." Does this sound the ultimate in impracticality and, well, really, just a little bit weird? I had difficulty with this until I began to seek the underlying meaning. In what way can the Lord be my husband? Well, what do I look for in a husband? One thing is strength — an arm to lean on or a shoulder to cry on, someone to tell me he loves me when I'm low. Can the Lord fill these requirements?

He can if His promises are true, if He is dependable.

Another thing I look for is an ability to take over, to plan. (Wouldn't it be nice to say, "You take care of this business matter; that's your department;" or "You decide where we go on vacation this year; I'm tired.") Can we, dare we, expect God to do this sort of thing for us? We can, and many of us can testify that He plans far better than we can — from finances to vacations.

And then, of course, there is companionship. It's a constant delight to me to see young Christians here experiencing the reality of the Lord's companionship. So often they face hard and frightening situations as they leave L'Abri, and yet the Holy Spirit teaches them in a surprisingly short time that He is real and that He does go with them. One of the verses they enjoy most is Hebrews 13:5 in the *Amplified Version:*

> "(God) Himself has said, I will not in any way fail you nor give you up nor leave you without support. [I will] not, [I will] not, [I will] not in any degree leave you helpless, *nor* forsake *nor* let [you] down . . . . Assuredly not!"

And tenderness? "For the Lord has called *you* as a woman forsaken and grieved in spirit." This is a promise of unique significance to those of us who are alone, who have experienced some of the bitterness of being forsaken or rejected or not chosen. The *Lord* has called us. There are heart promises that have a special glow for those who are alone, who share some of the loneliness He knew so well.

To many this could sound like escapism or, at best, sublimation, but I maintain that as we experience these things in depth, we are tasting the best of God's wine in having a personal relationship with the Lord of glory — a relationship that no human bond can ever equal for deep and total satisfaction. If one day He gives you a human partner, may it be a thing of richness and beauty enhanced with the special wonder a Christian marriage should have. But then, as now, may your relationship with the Lord Jesus Christ remain your top priority. It is for this we were made, and no other relationship can ever completely fill *all* our needs *all* the time.